CONTENTS

Introduction *4*

BACKGROUND
Geography *6*
History *8*
The Knights of St John 12
People and Culture *15*
The British Influence 18

EXPLORING MALTA
Must See *20*
Valletta *23*
City Gate to Upper Barracca
    Gardens *25*
A Walk Beside Grand Harbour
    28
Fort St Elmo *31*
Republic Street *32*
The Three Cities *39*
North of Valletta *45*
Sliema *45*
St Julian's Bay and St George's
    Bay *46*
South of Three Cities *48*
The South *51*
Marsaskala *52*
Marsaxlokk Bay *53*
The Southern Coastline *55*
Dingli Cliffs and Buskett
    Gardens *57*
Mdina and Rabat *58*

Naxxar *68*
The North *69*
Buġibba and St Paul's Bay *69*
Mellieħa Bay *72*
Marfa Ridge *72*
West Coast Beaches *74*
Historic Sites *75*
Mysteries in Stone 76
Gozo *78*
Comino *90*

ENJOYING YOUR VISIT
Weather *92*
Calendar of Events *92*
Accommodation *95*
Food and Drink *98*
Shopping *104*
Entertainment and Nightlife
    106
Sport *110*

A-Z FACTFINDER
The Basics *112*
A-Z Information *114*

Index *127*

INTRODUCTION

Situated at the very heart of the Mediterranean, it is little wonder that Malta has been fought over for centuries as a pawn in the game of world domination. Many islands may claim a similar fate, yet none have been so pivotal to world events – on two occasions – as Malta. In 1563 Malta's overlords, the Knights of St John, saved Christendom by heroically resisting the forces of Islam. Then during its second great siege in 1942 the island once again held firm, this time against the might of Hitler. As a consequence, the Allies went on to win North Africa. Churchill paid tribute to the significance of Malta's stand, describing the island as 'that tiny rock of history and romance'.

Today, northern European visitors come largely for Malta's glorious blue skies and even bluer waters. It is an island where summer sun is guaranteed, it is very reasonably priced and everything is in place for the holidaymaker. For British visitors in particular it is a comfortably reassuring destination, to which the legacy of Empire has bequeathed the English language, red telephone boxes and antique British vehicles driving on the left-hand side of the road. Providing exotic contrast are the typically Maltese high-prowed *luzzu* fishing boats, signed with the eye of Osiris to ward off evil.

For most package visitors, Malta is a very uncomplicated place to simply soak up the sun's rays. Yet it does have an historic past worthy of exploration. Valletta is the heart and history of Malta, built deliberately to impress by the Knights of St John over 400 years ago. Even today it is one of the architectural showpieces of the Mediterranean and one of the greatest fortified cities in the world. A tour around its bastions is unforgettable. Outside the capital, Malta's long and turbulent history is marked by its diverse cultural heritage. Mysterious Neolithic temples stretch back 5 000 years and represent some of the oldest of their kind to be found anywhere. The Knights of St John bequeathed impressive Baroque buildings and fortifications, and the island's beautiful, dominating churches reflect Malta's enduring Christian tradition.

Gozo is Malta as it used to be. No-one pretends Malta's tourist infrastructure has been developed in the best possible taste but on Gozo it has another chance, and so far the signs are good. It's well worth a visit, and a night or two away from the crowds on this greener, smaller island will probably leave you with a very different view of the Maltese archipelago.

The eye of Osiris looks on as the boat-builder renovates his luzzu.

GEOGRAPHY

Malta lies some 95km (60 miles) south of Sicily and 290km (180 miles) east of Tunisia, surrounded by some of the most pristine water in the Mediterranean. Malta is both the name of the main island and also the archipelago.

Malta, the island, is about 20km (13 miles) wide and 14km (9 miles) deep at its furthest points, though corner to corner it measures around 27km (17 miles). Neighbouring Gozo is 15km (9 miles) by 7km (4 miles) at its widest points but in total area is only just over one quarter the size of Malta. Comino covers just one square mile, while the remaining islets, Cominotto and Filfla are tiny uninhabited rocks.

Topographically Malta is somewhat featureless, consisting of a gently undulating limestone platform. There are no significant rivers or lakes, no mountains, and the highest point on the island is a very modest 253m (830ft), on the cliffs at Dingli. Malta's cliffs and bays are its most dramatic features. Dingli on Malta and Dwejra on Gozo are the most famous sites, though a helicopter trip will show you many other cliffs which drop in spectacular fashion down into the sea. The bays of Valletta have provided some of the best natural harbours in the world for fleets going back to the days of the Phoenicians, and are one of the principal reasons why so much attention has been paid to this tiny rock throughout history.

The land is badly denuded, deforested by early shipbuilders, and the forest of Buskett Gardens is the only significant survivor from this destruction. The only other trees on the island are those which have been planted in

A field of scarlet blooms brighten the arid landscape at Xlendi, Gozo.

parks and town squares.

The roadsides are peppered with rose laurel, while capers grow along walls and the honey-coloured buildings are adorned with bougainvillea and oleander. The landscape is broken with ginko trees, fig cactus and agaves, and on cultivated terraces you will see small plantations of olives, figs, oranges and lemons. Wild flowers abound in autumn, winter and spring, when the valleys are carpeted with colourful displays.

The islands are almost entirely made up of limestone and sandstone, quarried for centuries as building materials so that towns and villages, farms and even field walls have (until recently) had a harmonious honey-coloured appearance. Sadly, most recent

development has chosen to ignore this natural principle. Building development has exploded in the last three decades in Malta and there are few areas now that are untouched. Gozo is much less developed than Malta and, thanks to an underlying layer of clay which preserves the modest rainfall, is also greener. Comino, by contrast, is a barren, scorched, empty rock.

Beaches are not the island's forte, yet the waters around Malta are clean, clear and amazingly blue. There are plenty of rocky coves to swim from, but if you are in search of sand you will need to go to the north, to Mellieha and around Golden Bay.

HISTORY

Prehistory to the Romans

The Maltese islands have been inhabited for around 6 000 years, the most tangible early remains being the great stone temples which first began to appear around 3250 BC. The flint that the early Maltese used for their tools came from Sicily, and it was probably from here that the people also came. In fact, well before man came on the scene the islands were part of a land mass that joined southern Europe to northern Africa.

It was the **Phoenicians** who brought the first real civilisation to Malta around the 9C BC. This powerful trading nation from the east used Malta as a Mediterranean staging post and brought a degree of prosperity. They were succeeded by the **Carthaginians**, who were based just across the sea in present-day Tunisia. Their reign was less benign and for the first time Malta assumed a military strategic position and became embroiled in war. Following

Carthage's eventual defeat by the **Romans** in the Punic Wars, c 218 BC, the islands passed to the Romans who ruled them for the next 600 years.

St Paul

Despite the fact that the Romans established the basis for the present-day cities of Mdina on Malta and Victoria on Gozo, they largely ignored the islands and this period is most remembered for the arrival of **St Paul**. The apostle was shipwrecked just off the bay which now bears his name, while on his way to Rome in AD 60. He stayed on Malta for three months and, according to tradition, converted the Roman governor, Publius, to

This original mosaic floor at the Roman Villa Museum, Rabat, is one of the few signs of the Romans' 600-year presence on Malta.

Christianity. Whatever the truth of this, Christianity certainly took an early hold in the islands, as evidenced by Christian catacombs from the 2C.

With the fall of the Roman Empire Malta entered what seems to have been a fairly uneventful Dark Age, until its occupation by the **Arabs** in 870. They too left little mark, most notably expanding (and naming) Mdina. Their only lasting contribution was to *Malti*, the islanders' language, which even today contains many elements of Arabic.

The Knights of St John

In 1090 the Norman count, Roger of Sicily, forced the Arabs out of Malta and restored Christian rule. Over the next four centuries Malta became a pawn of the European powers, passing from Sicilian to French to Spanish hands by war, marriage or inheritance. Then in 1530 the Emperor Charles V of Spain made the momentous decision to grant the islands to the **Knights of the Order of St John**, who made their base at Birgu, now Vittoriosa.

After the **Great Siege** of 1565 (*see* pp.12-13), the Knights set to building a brand new fortified city. Resources were not a problem as the grateful countries of Europe lavished money and honours upon the Order and the Pope sent his chief engineer to supervise the work. Within the remarkably short space of five years the city of Valletta, named after the victorious siege commander, Grand Master La Valette, had taken shape.

The Order resumed its humanitarian vocation; the construction of the Hospital of St Elmo was undertaken, and was one of the most well-equipped in Europe at that time. In the afterglow of victory, Malta entered a brief golden age. The Grand Master was now on a par with European royalty and the Knights enjoyed an extravagant lifestyle. Ironically, with the defeat of Islam the Order lost its purpose and direction and it steadily slipped into decadence and corruption, concentrating all its energies on simply filling its own coffers.

French and British Rule

By the end of the 18C **Napoleon** had his eyes fixed on the island and in 1798 the once-proud Knights, by now bereft of courage, willpower and fighting practice, capitulated without firing a shot.

Napoleon abolished the Order and plundered their treasures. The Knights left Malta and installed themselves in Rome, where the Order continued to fufill humanitarian objectives throughout the world – even today the Order is present in more than 50 countries.

While the people of Malta were not unhappy to see the back of the Knights, they soon took exception to the **French rule** – in particular the ransacking of their beautiful churches – and revolted.

The **British** took the opportunity to help in the fight against their traditional rivals and in 1800 the French surrendered. Rather than risk the return of the Knights, the Maltese invited the British to stay. In 1814 Malta was formally recognised as a British colony by the Treaty of Paris. Under the British, Malta developed as an important strategic naval base, and the opening of the Suez Canal in 1869 further increased its importance as a trading port on the route to India.

The Knights of St John

The Knights of the Order of St John were formed on the pilgrim route to Jerusalem around the year 1000, dedicated to helping sick and exhausted travellers, and to protecting pilgrims from attack along the way. However, as the Crusades gathered pace and the Order began to attract recruits from some of Europe's most noble families, so their emphasis changed to a military role and eventually they became the standard bearers in the Christian fight against Islam.

The Knights were based in Rhodes for almost 200 years but were ousted in 1522 by the forces of the Turkish Ottoman Empire. In 1530 they were offered Malta as a base and grudgingly accepted. In return they paid a token rent in the form of one falcon per year.

Within 35 years the Turks were again upon them. And this time the stakes were much higher. If Malta should fall, then all of Europe was threatened. The Knights, expecting the onslaught, had fortified Birgu and Senglea and, at the tip of the peninsula where Valletta now stands, they had built Fort St Elmo. The Turkish forces were 30 000-40 000 strong, the Knights and Maltese counted just 9 000 men. **The Great Siege** of 1565 began on 18 May, with the merciless battering of Fort St Elmo. The Turks aimed to capture it within days, yet it held firm for over a month

Bottom: The Fall of St Elmo, during the Great Siege of 1565.

A crusader from the Knights of Malta exhibition, Mdina.

and cost the Turks an estimated 8 000 men. The Knights retreated to Fort St Angelo. After four bloody months, with just 600 defenders left, reinforcements finally arrived from Sicily, and the Turks, having lost around 30 000 men, retreated never to return. Malta, and the Knights, were celebrated as the saviours of Christendom.

The Second World War

During the Second World War, Malta's geographical position once again meant it was at the centre of a struggle for supremacy in the Mediterranean. The Allies used it as a base to attack supply convoys to Rommel's North African campaign, but because of its isolation, and with the enemy territory of Italy only 95km (60 miles) away, it was extremely difficult to defend.

The bombing of Malta began in 1940 with attacks by the Italian air force, but it was in 1942 that the island's **Second Great Siege** really started. Hitler, exasperated by Mussolini's failure to neutralise the island, sent in the Luftwaffe and during March and April the equivalent of twice the number of bombs dropped during the London Blitz rained down on the tiny island. Malta became the most bombed place on earth. The attack continued for 154 days and nights and (as in 1565) the Maltese were just a matter of days from capitulation. But in August a desperately needed relief convoy finally beat the German blockade and the tide turned. The fortitude of the Maltese was

'Faith', one of the three Gloster Gladiator aircraft that defended Malta in 1942, can be seen in the War Museum, Valletta.

recognised by Britain, who awarded the island the **George Cross** (the highest civilian award for gallantry in battle). Fortunately, the island's man-made and natural cave defences limited civilian casualties to only 1 600 (from a population of 250 000). A further 650 Maltese servicemen lost their lives. The Allies went on to win North Africa but, had Rommel been reinforced, it is quite likely that the campaign would have been lost and the whole direction of the war may have changed. Once again, the heroism of Malta had been pivotal to world events.

Independence

Malta finally achieved statehood in 1962 and full independence from Britain in 1964, though the two countries remained on friendly terms and Malta chose to maintain its close links for another 15 years. In 1974 the island became a **Republic**; in 1979 the last British forces finally sailed out of Malta for good. Malta hopes to join the European Community, and is preparing to meet the necessary requirements by 1 January 2003.

PEOPLE AND CULTURE

There is one thing that almost all visitors agree on: the Maltese are good hosts, and as long as you frequent places where Maltese people go then you will nearly always find a smile and good, old-fashioned courtesy. A good-natured rivalry exists between the Maltese and Gozitans, but both extend warm hospitality to visitors. Because of their close proximity to Italy you might expect the Maltese to be of Latin temperament. Yet in general they are more subdued, less flamboyant than their Latin cousins.

16

Throngs of Maltese gather at the foot of the Church of St Philip, Żebbug, to celebrate his saint's day.

Perhaps the Maltese have been practising too much British 'stiff upper lip' over the last two centuries (*see* p.18).

There are notable exceptions, however, when the Maltese do exhibit their southern European nature. On warm summer nights, most noticeably by the seafront, families come out for the evening *passegiata*, or promenade, just as they do all over Italy and Spain. Dressed for show, they chat to friends, eat ice creams, pause at kiosks for a Kinnie or a Hopleaf, perhaps stop off at a seafront pizzeria, wander back the way they came and return home. The casual visitor, seeing so many people gathered, often wonders what special event is going on. The Maltese also demonstrate their gregarious nature at Carnival time and during the festivals, which are a weekly feature of the Maltese summer calendar (*see* p.92).

Perhaps influenced by the nature of their existence on a small island, the Maltese are a tight-knit community, in which the family is of paramount importance. Look at the names above shops and businesses and the same ones recur: Azzopardi, Borg, Camilleri, Grech, Zammit and so on. Close family ties are reinforced by religion and some 80 per cent of Maltese still attend church regularly (numbers are declining among the young). No wonder then that there are so many large churches dotted around the island.

It is said jokingly that the proof that the Maltese believe in God is demonstrated by the way they drive. And not so long ago a popular island song coined the now-famous line about how they drive neither on the left or right, but in the shade. The accident statistics are no laughing matter, however, so be very careful as a driver and a pedestrian.

The British Influence

The British account for over 40 per cent of all Malta's tourists – and one of the reasons why they love it so much is because it is reassuringly familiar. The natives speak English, they drive on the left and they drink Hopleaf Pale Ale and shandy. Why, they are hardly foreign at all!

All this is a vestige of over 160 years of British rule. From the defeat of Napoleon until 1964 Malta belonged to Britain and became a vital strategic naval base which assumed global importance during the Second World War (*see* p.14). For most of Britain's rule the relationship between the two countries was cordial and when the British finally departed it was on very amicable terms.

For British visitors of a certain age, a trip to Malta is a walk down Memory Lane. Many of Malta's battered old cars – its Ford Anglias and Ford Prefects, Morris Minors, Hillman Imps and Austin Sevens – were the classic British production cars of the 1960s and early 1970s, while its buses go back beyond even

A policeman surveys a British-looking scene, Għarb, Gozo.

that era. Vintage Leylands, Bedfords and AECs chug around the island much as similar vehicles once chugged around the quiet lanes of towns and villages in post-war Britain. Then, as now, they passed shops with names such as Coronation Store, Economic Store and The Silver Jubilee. Other nostalgic street evidence of the British occupation, which is still in vogue here, are blue lamps above police stations and red telephone boxes.

Queen Victoria casts a regal eye over Republic Square, Valletta.

Many older visitors who were on armed service in Malta will certainly remember 'The Gut', (Strait Street) in Valletta. Once it throbbed with bars and nightclubs of ill-repute. With the departure of the British fleet it fell quiet and today it is all but finished, though a single male may well still be propositioned while walking along here.

Dinosaur of motoring, Leyland bus.

MUST SEE

Grand Harbour★★★,Valletta
The **harbour cruise**, which takes in Grand Harbour and Marsamxett Harbour, provides a memorable and scenic introduction to the history of this great city. Alternatively, you can walk the circular route around the mighty **ramparts**, which offer panoramic views across the waters where Malta's great battles were fought.

St John's Co-Cathedral★★★, Valletta
One of the greatest architectural monuments on the island, the austere façade belies the outstanding Baroque interior, with Caravaggio's masterpiece, *The Beheading of St John*.

Palace of the Grand Master★★,Valletta
Now the President's Palace, this 16C masterpiece of Gerolamo Cassar contains paintings, furniture, frescoes and decorations which date back to the times of the Knights of St John, while the **Armoury** is a showpiece of suits of armour and weapons.

Ħal Saflieni Hypogeum★★★ and the Tarxien Temples★★★
The huge underground complex of chambers of the **Hypogeum★★★**, dating from around 2 400 BC, were used for worship and burial, and

represent one of the holiest sites on the island. The nearby **Tarxien temples★★★** are richly embellished with carvings, and many of the finds are displayed in the **National Museum of Archaeology★★**, Valletta.

Blue Grotto★★

In early morning, before the sun is too high, explore the magnificent caves by boat, and marvel at the vivid blue waters.

The stunning, natural Grand Harbour, has been the stage for Malta's great battles.

Marsaxlokk★
The most picturesque fishing bay in Malta is
a riot of colour, thanks to its fleet of
traditional *luzzus*. Spend a perfect hour or
two with a lazy fish lunch on the quay.

Mdina★★
The old capital of Malta, this medieval city is
set right in the centre of the island; Bastion
Square and the city walls provide
magnificent far-reaching views. Explore its
narrow streets, packed tight with historic
gems – from the outstanding Baroque
Cathedral of St Peter and St Paul★★ to tiny
piazzas. Wander its streets, enjoy its peaceful,
restrained atmosphere and understand how
it came to be called the 'Silent City'.

St Paul's and St Agatha's Catacombs★★,
Rabat
The extensive labyrinth of underground
burial chambers under Rabat were hewn
from the rocks in the Christian era. St
Agatha was said to have hidden here in
AD 249 before returning to Sicily where she
was martyred.

Mosta Dome★★
The parish church of Mosta has one of the
largest unsupported church domes in the
world, and can be seen from miles around.

Gozo★
Most visitors to Malta make the short ferry
trip to the greener, more peaceful island of
Gozo, whose attractions include the
Citadel★, **Cathedral★** and museums of
Victoria★, the prehistoric temples of
Ġgantija★★★ and excellent diving in the
sparkling, azure waters.

VALLETTA★★★

The Mediterranean sun imbues the steeple of St Paul's Anglican Cathedral and the magnificent dome of Valletta's Carmelite Church with a golden glow.

'A city built by gentlemen for gentlemen', Valletta is not only the pride of Malta but one of the world's great fortified cities. Constructed by the Knights of St John in the immediate aftermath of the Great Siege of 1565 (*see* p.12), its enormous complex of defences were built to ensure that never again would the Turks threaten Malta. Many

of the forts and huge bastions which protect
the city occupy the area across Grand
Harbour known as the Three Cities, though
the original fortification of St Elmo is at the
very tip of Valletta itself. Before you even set
foot in Valletta it's a good idea to take a
harbour cruise (regular departures from
Sliema, *see* p.106), which will give you an
informative commentary and an invader's-
eye view of Valletta's formidable defences.

The usual way of arriving in Valletta is
aboard one of the island's bone-shaker buses
which judder to a halt immediately outside

*Charming stepped
streets make
discovering Valletta a
decidedly pedestrian
experience.*

the main gate. Don't think of driving in Valletta; the streets are narrow and cramped, with very little parking space, but, as long as you don't mind lots of steps, the city is made for walking.

There are scores of delightful local vignettes and architectural details to enjoy amid its handsome balconied golden sandstone houses and shops, and its strict grid pattern makes navigation easy and offers tantalising sea views along its straight, narrow streets. Moreover, as capital cities go, it is small – from end to end takes no more than 20 minutes on foot. If the walking does get tiring you can always hail a *karrozin* (horse-drawn cab), which make various sightseeing circuits of Valletta. A walk along the imposing ramparts provides splendid views over Grand Harbour, where Malta's historic battles were staged. A leisurely stroll, with breaks at some of the open-air bars and cafés along the way, takes a couple of hours. You can just about cover the main sights of Valletta in a day, but you'll probably want to take longer.

City Gate to Upper Barracca Gardens

First impressions of Valletta are inauspicious. By any standards the entrance square is a mess and the area just beyond looks like a bomb site. In fact it *is* a bomb site – all that remains of the old **Opera House**, left in ruins since its destruction in 1942. Millennium plans are afoot for conversion to a cultural centre.

By way of contrast, head off right, along South Street, to see one of Malta's finest buildings, the splendid **Auberge de Castille et León★**, formerly home to one of the Spanish *langues* of the Knights of St John. A

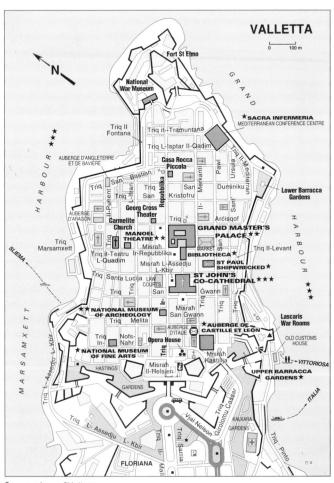

Street plan of Valletta

Constructed in 1574, the Auberge de Castille et León has housed Spanish Knights, the British Army and currently the Prime Minister, all behind its Baroque façade. Maltese writer Manuel Dimech is immortalised in the gardens.

langue was a national or regional grouping of the Knights of St John. In all there were eight: Angleterre (England), Auvergne, Provence, France, Aragon, Castille, Germany and Italy. Each langue had its own *auberge* (literally, an inn) which was similar to a traditional English university college providing accommodation, a chapel and a dining hall, built around a courtyard. The Auberge de Castille et León is the finest surviving example of this institution, and is now home to the Prime Minister's office (no entry to the public).

A few metres away are the very popular **Upper Barracca Gardens★**. This relaxed leafy area, with its fountains, ducks, sculptures and outdoor café, offers wonderful **views★★** over Grand Harbour from its elevated position. Adjacent to the gardens is the entrance to the **Sacred Island** film show which takes a look at Malta's history from a Christian perspective. Of more general interest are the fascinating **Lascaris War Rooms**, a subterranean labyrinth of rooms which served as operations HQ during the Second World War. It is fully 'staffed' by life-sized figures and reconstructions; an audio-tour fills in the details (open Mon-Fri 9.30am-4pm; Sat, Sun 9.30am-12.30pm).

An oasis of foliage and shade, Upper Barracca Gardens afford spectacular views of the Grand Harbour.

A Walk Beside Grand Harbour

Follow the harbourside road, Triq Il-Levant (East Street), straight downhill, enjoying the sea views, and make a brief diversion along

Triq Santa Lucija to the **Church of St Paul Shipwrecked★**. This tiny church, with its Maltese Baroque façade, is one of Valletta's hidden gems. Built to commemorate St Paul's arrival in Malta, almost every square inch of the interior is richly decorated.

Ornate and exhuberant, the Church of St Paul Shipwrecked reputedly contains one of the saint's arm bones.

Return to East Street, which continues along the harbourside as Triq Il-Mediterran, past **Lower Barracca Gardens** to the **Malta Experience★**. This is the best of Malta's many audio-visual shows and provides a

Market stalls and eager shoppers pack this street in Valletta.

comprehensive and entertaining introduction to the island, compressing its 7 000-year history into 45 minutes (shows Mon-Fri hourly from 11am-4pm; Sat, Sun hourly from 11am-1pm).

Adjacent is the **Sacra Infermeria**★ (the Holy Infirmary), which the Knights built as a hospital in 1574. Its handsome Long Hall, formerly the hospital ward containing a staggering 563 beds, stretches a very impressive 155m (509ft). The building's new role is as the Mediterranean Conference Centre but the Long Hall is open to the public, subject to functions. Housed below the Sacra Infermeria is the **Knights Hospitallers**★, a lively exhibition of tableaux which relates not only the history of the building but the Knights' original functions as hospitallers, complete with authentic sights, sounds and smells (open Mon-Fri 9.30am-4.30pm; Sat, Sun 9.30am-1.30pm).

Fort St Elmo

On the very tip of the peninsula stands **Fort St Elmo**. This star-shaped fortress, built in 1552, was at the very heart of the Great Siege and its terrible hand-to-hand fighting (*see* pp.12-13). On 23 June 1565, after 31 days of siege, its 600 survivors were finally overpowered and slaughtered by the Turks. Every other Sunday (weather permitting) a spectacular live historical re-enactment of a military parade, called **In Guardia!**, is staged here (*see* p.108). This is the best show on the island, full of colour, explosions and the smell of gunpowder. Don't miss it. Afterwards an excellent guided tour of the fort is conducted. St Elmo is also open when *In Guardia!* is not on (Sat 1-5pm, Sun 9am-5pm, tours hourly). Another part of St Elmo (different entrance) houses the **National War Museum**. The highlights of this small collection are the island's George Cross and part of *Faith*, one of the three aircraft which

Fort St Elmo, with the Siege Bell commemorating the dead of the Second World War, guards the harbour entrance with Fort Ricasoli opposite.

valiantly defended Malta in 1942 (*see* p.14).
It's a good idea to visit the Wartime
Experience (*see* p.34) before coming here,
to appreciate the exhibits fully.

Republic Street (Triq Ir-Repubblika)
Head back towards the City Gate on
Republic Street, Valletta's handsome main
thoroughfare. At no 74 is the **Casa Rocca
Piccola**, the small 16C home of a Maltese
noble family (who still live here) and the
only one of its kind open to the public in
Valletta. A member of the family leads a
lively guided tour (open daily, except Sun).

A little further along is the **Grand Master's
Palace★★**, built in 1571 to designs by Malta's
outstanding architect, Gerolamo Cassar, and
occupied by every Grand Master until the
Order left Malta in 1798. From 1814 it
became the official residence of the British
Governor and since 1974 it has been the
office of the President of Malta.

Within the Palace are two courtyards,
Neptune Court and Prince Alfred Court,
where you can rest in the shaded greenery
between tours of the Palace's main
attractions for visitors – the Armoury and
the Apartments. The **Armoury** represents a
splendid collection, bristling with some
6 000 pieces of weaponry and armour,
including the gold inlaid suit made for the
French Grand Master Wignacourt
(1610-20). The **Apartments**, approached
along atmospheric corridors lined with suits
of armour, are also a treat. Guided tours
include the Tapestry Room, the Throne
Room, the Hall of the Ambassadors and the
State Dining Room, where you can marvel at
the wonderful Gobelins tapestries, the
friezes and frescoes recalling the heroic

*16C sentries guard
the cool, imposing
corridors of the
Grand Master's
Palace.*

deeds of the Knights of St John and the grandeur of the decor and furniture.

On the square opposite the palace is the George Cross Theatre which alternates two audio-video shows. Complete with sensurround sound, the self-explanatory **Valletta Experience** illustrates the history of the city 'built for gentlemen by gentlemen' (shows Mon-Fri 10am, noon, 2pm; Sat 10am, noon). The **Malta George Cross – The Wartime Experience** is a stirring account of Malta's Second Great Siege of 1942 (shows Mon-Fri 10am, 2pm; Sat 10pm).

Adjacent to the Palace is **Republic Square** (Misraħ Ir-Repubblika) which is also known as **Queen's Square** as it is dedicated to Queen Victoria, though you may have to look for her statue through a forest of sunshades which mark the patch of the **Caffe Cordina**, Valletta's best-known watering hole. Look inside at its beautiful painted ceiling by Giuseppe Cali. Also on

Once stage to opera, comedy, tragedy, dance and film, the 18C gilded Manoel Theatre has discovered a new lease of life.

the square is the **National Library★** (Bibliotheca), an elegant building designed to house the Knights' archives. It exhibits many valuable historical documents, books and manuscripts, and is well worth a quick visit, particularly as there is no charge for entrance.

Head off Republic Square, alongside Marks & Spencer, to the **Manoel Theatre★★**, built in 1731 by the Grand Master Manoel de Vilhena. It is one of Europe's oldest and quaintest theatres and you certainly don't have to be a fan of the stage to enjoy a guided tour of its restored gilded and painted interior (Mon-Fri 10.30am, 11.30am; Sat 11.30am). Across the street is the **Carmelite Church**, a Valletta landmark famous for its huge dome, and best appreciated from across the water in Sliema. Its light and airy interior is a delight, even though it was completely rebuilt after the Second World War.

The sandstone dome of the Carmelite Church dominates the skyline of Marsamxett Harbour.

Return to Republic Street and beside the next square, **Great Siege Square** (Misrah L-Assedju L-Kbir) is Malta's principal church, **St John's Co-Cathedral★★★**. Its plain, austere exterior belies an interior which is a sculpted, gilded and decorated extravaganza. It was built by Girolamo Cassar between 1573 and 1577 for the Knights, and was decorated a hundred years later following the designs of Mattia Preti, and is quite unusual in that everything within it has been made especially for the church.

Mattia Preti's exquisite interior overwhelms the visitor to St John's Co-Cathedral.

Concealed behind the prosaic façade of St John's Co-Cathedral, Baroque artistry runs amok.

Many of the Knights for whom the cathedral was built still lie here beneath the 400 or so colourful **tomb slabs** upon which you cannot help but stand. They are a history book in themselves, documenting European history of the 17-18C, as they represent the great families of the different countries from which the Knights came. Twelve Grand Masters, including city founder La Valette, also lie below you, in the crypt (not open to the public). The **ceiling** and most of the altar paintings in the chapels represent important works of

Mattia Preti.

The cathedral's greatest treasures are the powerful *Beheading of John the Baptist* (now re-installed in the Cathedral's oratory after nearly three years of restoration in Florence) and in the **museum** the studious *St Jerome*, both by Caravaggio. There's also a large and opulent collection of ecclesiastical objects and huge Flemish tapestries to see.

Back on Republic Street you'll find the **National Museum of Archaeology**★★ housed in the former Auberge de Provence, built in 1571. If you are visiting Malta for its prehistoric sites this is absolutely invaluable, as you can stock up on all the information that you will find lacking at the actual sites. Here you will find excellent displays of the rich archaeological exhibits from Malta's Neolithic sites and it also includes Bronze and Iron Age and Roman finds. Highlights include the famous *Venus of Malta* and the *Sleeping Priestess*, found in the Hypogeum (*see* p.50). Huge stone slabs from the temples, dating from the 3C BC and decorated with spiral motifs, are displayed on the ground floor. The museum is scheduled to expand by the end of 1999 to include a Bronze Age wing and a Punic and Roman wing.

Near the top of Republic Street turn along Triq Nofs-In-Nhar (South Street) for the **National Museum of Fine Arts**★. Housed in an attractive Baroque palace built by the Knights in the 16C, the collection includes 14C-17C Italian paintings and a significant array of Maltese works. Much of its space is devoted to religious subjects. The highlight is probably the works of Mattia Preti (1613-99), who was responsible for the decoration of St John's Co-Cathedral.

Who can guess the dreams of the 'Sleeping Priestess'? A strangely moving sculpture from the dawn of history.

THE THREE CITIES★★

The famous Three Cities, best viewed from the Upper Barracca Gardens in Valletta, are **Vittoriosa★★** (Birgu), **Senglea** (L'Isla) and **Cospicua** (Bormla), though the latter has little sightseeing interest. The boat trip which takes in Grand Harbour is a must to view their sea defences. There is a Vintage Bus service (departs from Sliema by the ferries) which tours this area with a commentary, but note that it does not stop en route. A better bet is simply to jump

A dgħajsa (ferryboat) idly pulls across Senglea's waterfront.

aboard a bus from Valletta (nos 1, 2 or 6 to
Vittoriosa or no 3 to Senglea) and find your
own way around. The Three Cities are also
known as **The Cottonera** or Cottonera Lines,
named after the defences initiated by Grand
Master Cottonera in 1670 which protect
them. The tourist office has a useful *Walking
Tour of the Cottonera* leaflet. In summer a
traditional Maltese ferry boat known as a
dghajsa (pronounced dicer) runs between
Vittoriosa and Senglea.

Vittoriosa★★

After passing through **Cospicua**, an earthy
dockside area, you enter the peninsula that
Vittoriosa occupies. Of the Three Cities, it is
the least changed – take time to explore its
narrow alleys and streets, where fine stone
balconies adorn the houses and other
architectural gems await discovery. Birgu was
the original name of this area, which formed
the base of the Knights of St John up to
1565. It only acquired its new name
(meaning Victorious) after the Great Siege.

Situated at the tip of the peninsula is the
pride of Vittoriosa, the mighty **Fort St
Angelo**, the Knights' headquarters and
command centre during the Great Siege
after the fall of Fort St Elmo. Only recently
re-opened to the public, there is not a lot to
see here, but the **views★★** of Grand Harbour
make the effort worthwhile. Pick up a self-
guided walking tour leaflet from the Valletta
tourist office.

Enjoying a splendid setting overlooking
the Dockyard Creek is the imposing
Baroque **Church of St Lawrence★**. Built in
the 16C, this was the Knights' conventual
church and although the present building is
a reconstruction of the original, relics of the

Order, including Grand Master La Valette's hat and sword, may be seen in the museum behind the church (erratic opening hours, enquire at the Valletta tourist office). The church itself has a richly-decorated interior, including Mattia Preti's fine altarpiece, *The Martyrdom of St Lawrence*. In front of St Lawrence is the **Freedom Monument**, which marks the spot where in 1979 the British finally handed the island back to the Maltese people.

Behind the church is **Vittoriosa Square**, and off here is Main Gate Street where you will find the **Palazzo del Sant'Uffizio**★★ (Inquisitor's Palace). Used by the dreaded Inquisition from 1574 to 1798, even today

The Inquisitor's Palace, where the authority of the Church was exercised to the full.

the low door forces visitors to bow in submission upon entry to the Judgement Room. The Inquisitor, appointed to defend the Catholic faith against heresy, often abused his powerful position and was unpopular with both the Knights and the Maltese. You can tour some of the grand rooms of the palace, and also the cells where the graffiti of hapless interns of the Inquisition still remains. Contrary to popular myth, however, there are no records of torture here.

Also off Vittoriosa Square is Britannic (Hilda Tabone) Street, the headquarters of the Knights, where many of their auberges are to be found. It's still a handsome street and plaques locate some of the long-gone auberges. Take the first turn right into North West/Mistral Street and you can enter the charming building which used to house

The Maritime Museum marks Malta's seafaring exploits from the days of the Knights.

All eyes and ears – Senglea Vedette (lookout turret), guards Grand Harbour, looking towards Valletta.

The deep blue of the water against honey-coloured walls, the domes and bell towers rising skyward; whether viewed from the ancient ramparts or from a ship's deck, the panorama of Grand Harbour will take your breath away.

the former **Auberge d'Angleterre** and is now a public library (open Mon-Sat 7.30am-1.30pm summer; 8.30am-4.30pm winter).

Return to the church and on the dockside in the handsome colonnaded building that used to house the Naval Bakery is now the **Maritime Museum★**. It's an entertaining collection, with actual ship sections, lots of models and other naval memorabilia.

Senglea

Directly opposite Vittoriosa lies Senglea, formerly named **L'Isla** (The Islet) and renamed in honour of Grand Master Claude de la Sengle. There are a handful of bars and sandwich stops along its waterfront and the **views★★** across to Vittoriosa, particularly

in the evening as the setting sun turns the sandstone into glowing gold, make a trip well worthwhile. At the very point, situated in the small but delightful **Gardjola Garden**, is the famous **Senglea Vedette** (lookout turret) with its symbols of vigilance – a large carved ear and an eye. As from Vittoriosa, the **views★★** across Grand Harbour to Valletta are tremendous.

Here's looking at you – Senglea's fine architecture and working docks.

NORTH OF VALLETTA

Sliema

Occupying a peninsula with seafronts on the Mediterranean and Marsamxett Harbour (pronounced mar-sam-shett), **Sliema** has long been one of Malta's most fashionable addresses. The centre is purely residential, though its coastal roads are now very touristy. From the harbour front, **boat trips** run around Grand Harbour, around the island, and to Comino. Here too is the landing stage for ferries across to Valletta, not as fast, but with excellent views and more relaxing than going by bus.

Towards the tip of the peninsula, by the Hotel Fortina, look across to see one of Malta's most photographed views – Valletta, in all her golden glory, with the dome of the Carmelite Church looking just like St Paul's Cathedral, London. Along the harbour front are some good cafés and bars, which are always thronged with visitors and locals alike.

In the middle of the harbour lies **Manoel Island**, connected by bridge to the mainland. The Phoenician Glassblowers Factory draws a steady stream of visitors; the rest of the island is devoted to boat repairs. The road continues round to **Msida Creek** (pronounced im-see-dah), a picturesque marina adorned by the pretty church of St Joseph. If it is *festa* time, don't miss the chance to see the church illuminated.

Sliema's Mediterranean aspect is **Tower Road** (Triq-it-Torri), an apt name given the high-rise blocks that have all but displaced the traditional stone houses and so disfigured its appearance. It's a lively holiday area nonetheless. The smooth rocks by the Hotel Preluna are a popular bathing area, and all along here there is a busy *passegiata* (promenade) on summer evenings, as groups pass from one seafront food and drink kiosk to the next. The only point of historical interest is the old **fortress**, also by the Preluna, now converted to a restaurant.

St Julian's Bay and St George's Bay

St Julian's (San Ġiljan) and St George's (San Gorg) are holiday-land, famous for the nightlife of Paceville. Its entrance however, **Spinola Bay**, is as pretty and romantic a place as you will see anywhere in Malta, clinging bravely to its fishing village heritage. The boathouses which are now home to the restaurants Caffe Raffael and

Fishing is still central to the lives many Maltese, and fishermen unload their brightly painted boats in Spinola Bay.

San Giuliano (*see* p.102) once belonged to the grand **Spinola Palace** estate. The Palace, built in 1688, still stands and is also now a restaurant, set in lovely grounds on the hill behind the boathouses. You'll have to turn up very early on a summer's evening to get front row seats overlooking Spinola Bay at any of the establishments which line the waterfront here, but it's worth the effort.

Directly behind St Julian's is **Paceville** (pronounced par-chay ville), with a multitude of restaurants specialising in a wide variety of cuisines, nightspots aimed at the youth market, and countless bars. Some of this spills over into St George's Bay, where there are also 5-star hotels and the

Alongside the fishermen, tourist activity is centred on St Julian's and Spinola Bay.

Dragonara Hotel Casino. There is a small, sheltered sandy beach at St George's.

South of the Three Cities

Head south from Vittoriosa towards Żabbar and you will leave the city through the monumental **Żabbar Gate**, one of the finest gateways constructed along the Cottonera Lines. It is not so spectacular on the Vittoriosa face, so you will have to look back to enjoy its detail. In the centre of the town

Majestic Żabbar Gate marks the entrance to the Three Cities.

stop to admire the parish church, the
Sanctuary of the Virgin of Grace★, with its
collection of *ex voto* paintings in the museum
next door. Begun in 1641, it is one of Malta's
most glorious Baroque creations and the
focal point for many pilgrims. Head due
west towards Figura and Paola, and on a
roundabout you will see the **Hompesch
Arch**, dedicated to the very last Grand
Master, Ferdinard de Hompesch. It was the
last monument built by the Knights.

The dull, cramped suburb of Paola is
home to two of Malta's most important
temple complexes. The **Tarxien Temples★★★**
date back between 3 800 and 5 000 years,
and are most famous for the base of a giant
goddess statue. The rest of the piece, which
would have resembled a giant Mother Earth
figure, has sadly never been found. The
original is in the National Museum of
Archaeology in Valletta. Unfortunately, it is

*The Tarxien Temples
hint at Malta's
ancient past,
boasting one of the
earliest images of a
deity.*

difficult to visualise the temples from what remains, and the impact of the site is much reduced by its suburban setting. Try to visit the National Museum of Archaeology first to appreciate the temple complex as a whole, as well as to see the original finds.

A far better general sightseeing alternative is the **Ħal Saflieni Hypogeum★★★** (hypogeum simply means underground chamber). You have to descend some 12m (40ft) into the rock to enter this amazing temple, which comprises a labyrinth of chambers on three different levels, cut from the rock 4 000-5 000 years ago. It was used as a place of worship and of burial – the bones of over 7 000 people have been discovered. Items found here suggest the worship of a fertility cult and may also be seen in the National Museum of Archaeology, Valletta. A number of these relics support the hypothesis that it was also a training place for priestesses. Ironically, its oracle chamber has acoustics which will reverberate a deep male voice but not that of a female.

The temple features some fine carvings and was once probably the island's most sacred site. Because of its underground location it is also the only one of Malta's temples to have retained its roof. All traces of the people who built the Hypogeum vanish around 2000 BC. However, as this type of structure is unique in the world, little more is known of its function or usage.

Closed since 1991 for restoration, the Hypogeum reopened in September 2000, one of the greatest events in Malta to mark the new millennium. Access is controlled to limit the number of visitors at any one time in order to preserve the site, now classified by UNESCO.

Popular with locals, Marsaskala offers inviting cafés and lively evening entertainment.

THE SOUTH

The south of Malta holds two of the island's most picturesque and visited places, namely the pretty fishing village of Marsaxlokk (pronounced marcer-shlock) and the beautiful Blue Grotto. Close by are some of the island's best ancient sites – a huge cave with prehistoric animal remains and temples on cliff tops by the sea.

Few can resist the transluscent, cool waters of Peter's Pool.

Marsaskala (Wied-Il-Għajn)

The village-town of Marsaskala stretches around its long, indented bay and makes an unlikely resort, though it is very popular with domestic visitors who flock to its lively nightlife at weekends. There are always

Fleets of fishing boats pepper Marsaxlokk Bay, which retains its charm, despite the influx of tourists.

colourful boats at anchor in Marsaskala Bay, which with its Venetian-style campanile is an attractive sight. At the tip of the headland is the ironic juxtaposition of the prestigious Libyan-sponsored Jerma Palace Hotel and St Thomas Tower, built by the Knights of St John in 1614 to repel Islamic invaders.

Adjacent, **St Thomas's Bay** (Il-Bajja ta'San Tumas) is a jumble of tumble-down fishermen's huts and, not immediately apparent, a small sandy cove a short walk around the bay which is popular for swimming.

The area's most favoured bathing spot is **Peter's Pool**, which lies a few kilometres due south (though you'll have to drive inland first to reach it). There is no sand here but wind and waves have chiselled out a beautiful natural lido, with smooth rocks on which to recline next to sparkling blue waters. There are no facilities so bring your own food and drink. Beware, too, that Peter's Pool attracts petty thieves so never leave anything unattended in your car. The locals leave their car windows open so they are not smashed to force entry.

Shadows of prehistoric man lurk in Għar Dalam, the Cave of Darkness.

Marsaxlokk Bay
(Il Bajja ta'Marsaxlokk)
Marsaxlokk★ is famous as Malta's most picturesque fishing village and so attracts visitors by the coach load. They come to look at the harbour, chock full of brilliantly coloured *luzzus* (traditional Maltese fishing boats), the market, where lace tablecloths are the main

attraction, and, best of all, to sit outside by the quay enjoying an inexpensive fish lunch. Crowds aside, Marsaxlokk is essentially unchanged, and is refreshingly free of tourist hotels and souvenir shops.

Around the headland just before **Birżebbuġa** (pronounced beer-tsay-boo-jah) is the prehistoric cave of **Għar Dalam★★** (Cave of Darkness) where Neolithic man lived some 7 000 years ago. It has a large, wide, low entrance which you can walk into for some 80m (262ft), with display boards which tell you about the finds that were made here. The most interesting of these, several hundred animal fossils, including dwarf elephants and dwarf hippopotami, are exhibited in a small museum on site.

Sharing Marsaxlokk Bay is the alluring

Huge fossilised bones of prehistoric animals found at Għar Dalam are displayed at the museum.

Shades of turquoise and spectacular scenery at the Blue Grotto.

promise of a sandy beach at Birżebbuġa's **Pretty Bay**. Don't be misled. It certainly must have been pretty 15 years ago but now, almost within swimming distance of the beach, the presence of a huge containerised freeport, with giant cranes, an oil terminal and thousands of cargo ships per year, makes the name sadly inappropriate.

The Southern Coastline

The jewel of the southern coast is the **Blue Grotto**★★ , where pristine aquamarine waters lap around cliffs, coves, archways and caves. Small government-licensed and price-controlled sightseeing boats offer 25-minute tours around the caves, shuttling to and fro non-stop daily in summer (boats depart from the harbour of Wied iż-Żurrieq). The eponymous Blue Grotto is set some 50m (164ft) deep into the cliff side. The best time to visit is early in the morning on a calm, sunny day when the sun is sufficiently low to penetrate the caves. Also, the quieter and brighter the water, the more spectacular the viewing.

Just a few kilometres east lay the adjacent temples of **Haġar Qim***** (pronounced ha-jah eem) and **Mnajdra**** (im-na-ee-dra). Both date from around 3000-2500 BC. Haġar Qim, whose name means 'standing stones', is the more impressive of the two, featuring giant slabs, one measuring 7m by 3m (23ft by 10ft), and where you are free to roam inside. A long footpath descends from here, almost to the edge of

Haġar Qim's megaliths.

Shaded walk, Buskett Gardens.

the cliff top, to Mnajdra. This is in a better state of preservation than Ħaġar Qim but sadly is fenced off, so viewing is restricted. It is thought that its spectacular cliff-top setting is linked to the uninhabited islet of Filfla, 5km (3 miles) offshore.

Continue east and turn back to the sea to find the cove of **Għar Lapsi**. Like Peter's Pool, this is a picturesque rocky spot ideal for swimming. It's very popular with locals and has a basic café for refreshments.

Dingli Cliffs and Buskett Gardens

Dingli Cliffs are the most spectacular natural part of Malta's whole coastline, tumbling steeply to the Mediterranean from a height of over 250m (820ft). There's a viewpoint looking out to Filfla around 1.5km (1 mile) west of the Madalena Chapel on the highest point, and this whole stretch makes dramatic walking country. The village of Dingli, the highest on the island, is surrounded by a series of terraced fields set on the cliff tops.

A little way inland is **Buskett Gardens**, a bit of a misnomer as this is an area mostly devoted to woods and citrus groves. This delightful green and tranquil area is most popular with locals and tourists in spring, when everything is in blossom. At any time of year it's a pleasant place for a shady picnic (there's also a restaurant providing snacks) and comes alive at the festival of *Mnarja* each June (*see* p.93).

Delightfully situated overlooking the verdant Buskett Gardens is **Verdala Palace★★**, built in 1586 as a summer residence for Grand Master de Verdalle. Subsequently turned into a moated and fortified residence, today it is the summer house of the Maltese President. Part of the impressive interior is open to the public except during August (and sometimes also during September) when it is used to host visiting dignitaries. As it is set on the highest part of the island, there are splendid **views**★★ from the palace (open Tue and Fri 9am-noon, 2-5pm). Nearby you may spot through the trees another grand summer residence, the **Inquisitor's Summer Palace**, built in 1625. Now the Prime Minister's residence, it is closed to the public.

MDINA AND RABAT

Mdina, the old capital of Malta, is one of the island's gems. Here in the narrow streets and alleyways is a tangible sense of history. Immediately outside this citadel, a mere 5-10 minutes' walk away, is the town of Rabat, the commercial hub of central Malta. It is buzzing in comparison to Mdina, though sleepy too for much of the time, and home to Malta's finest catacombs.

Mdina★★

Mdina takes its name from the Arabs (a corruption of *Medina*, simply meaning 'the city'), who held Malta from 870 to 1090. The advantages which the Arabs saw in the city, a high fortified position in the centre of the island, surrounded by fertile agricultural land, also attracted the Knights of St John, and under them it took on the title *Citta Notabile* (The Eminent City). After the Knights moved to Valletta it fell, literally, quiet and became known as 'the Silent City'. Today, thanks to tourism it is no longer silent and although visiting cars are banned, residents' vehicles do disturb the historic

Mdina's mellow architecture remains little changed from its days as an Arabic stronghold.

Fall under the spell of hushed, time-worn streets straight from the pages of The Arabian Nights.

slumber. Nearly all of Mdina's sightseeing interest lies along its main street, **Triq Villegaignon★**, but the visitor who wants to discover the 'real Mdina' should take time to wander through the narrow, winding alleyways leading off here. Restored medieval houses, Baroque façades in mellow golden stone, adorned with stone or wrought iron balconies and intricate architectural details make Mdina a delight to explore.

There are still only a handful of restaurants and shops but there has been a recent outbreak of visitor attractions, in various forms of waxworks, tableaux and

audio-visuals, which attempt to capitalise on Mdina's heritage. A multimedia show which provides a good general introduction is **The Mdina Experience**. Signed off the Triq Villegaignon, it is in a medieval patrician's house on Mesquita Square (open Mon-Fri 10.30am-4pm; Sat 10.30am-2pm). Further along Triq Villegaignon is **Medieval Times**, in which scenes from medieval life are depicted (open Mon-Sat 9.30am-9.30pm; Sun 9.30am-8pm; reduced price tickets if also visiting the Mdina Experience). In Magazines Street, in the west of the city, the gunpowder vault in the battlements of Mdina are the setting for **The Knights of Malta**. A combination of life-sized models, tableaux and a multi-language commentary,

One of the three city gates which will admit you, perhaps by horse-drawn karrozin, *into the 'Silent City'.*

augmented with lighting, sound effects and smells, tells the story of the Knights in Mdina (open Mon-Fri 10.30am-4pm; Sat 10.30am-3pm).

As you enter the handsome main city gate across the dry moat, immediately on your right is the **Mdina Dungeons**. Set in real dungeons, this is an exhibition of medieval Maltese horror, a factually accurate and graphically disturbing trawl through episodes of the island's darker side (open June-Sept 10am-6.30pm; Oct-May 10am-5.30pm). It is not for the squeamish or young children. Adjacent is the handsome **Vilhena Palace★**, home to the small and old-fashioned **Museum of Natural History**. Concerts are held here as part of 'Malta fest' every year.

Back on Triq Villegaignon, pause awhile to look up and admire the façades of the various *palazzi* which adorn it, such as Casa Inguanez, Testaferrata Palace and Banca Giuratale. Halfway along is St Paul's Square,

Rebuilt from the rubble of the 1693 earthquake, the Cathedral of St Peter and St Paul.

dominated by the **Cathedral of St Peter and
St Paul★★**. The rich Baroque interior is one
of the finest in Malta, and most experts rate
it second only to St John's Co-Cathedral in
Valletta. Designed by the Maltese architect,
Lorenzo Gafà between 1697 and 1707, the
massive dome is Mdina's landmark. After
admiring the impressive façade, step into its
cool interior where the frescoes show scenes
from the life of St Paul. Also look for the
carved oak sacristy door and the magnificent
marble sepulchral slabs. The adjacent
Cathedral Museum★ includes religious art
and sacred exhibits, Roman antiquities and
fine paintings and engravings, including
works by some famous Old Masters such as
Dürer and Rembrandt.

Almost at the very end of the street is the
Palazzo Falzon★, also known as the Norman
House. This is the only *palazzo* in Mdina
which is open to the public (open Mon-Fri

*Roof frescoes depict
scenes from the life
of St Paul, an awe-
inspiring feat of
vertiginous artistry,
Cathedral of St
Peter and St Paul.*

9am-1pm, 2-4.30pm, subject to staff availability). It's a beautifully restored aristocratic house which reflects the domestic style of the mid-16C when Mdina was at its peak, and includes museum-style collections of pictures, pottery and everyday items.

Triq Villegaignon saves the best until last, and at the very end is **Bastion Square** whose city ramparts offer the best inland **views** in all Malta. You can see right across the giant dome of Mosta's church all the way to Valletta, and almost right along both coasts to St Paul's Bay and Marsaskala. On a clear day they say you can even spot Mount Etna on Sicily. As a bonus there are two charming tea rooms, both with grandstand seats al fresco on the terrace (*see* p.119).

Tucked away in the narrow streets of Mdina are hidden gems, such as this statue and decorated façade.

The marble statue in St Paul's Grotto originally came from Rhodes, where it was sculpted by Bernini, Michelangelo's assistant.

Rabat★

During Roman times, both Rabat and Mdina were a single city. The Arabs divided the two by means of a ditch, and Rabat became the suburb to the city of Mdina. Since then it has expanded and developed as a town in its own right, and there is much to delight the visitor who takes the time to explore its characterful streets.

Just outside the Mdina citadel is the **Roman Villa Museum**. Only a fine mosaic floor survives from the original villa, which was discovered in 1881 (*see* p.9). The reconstructed building contains Roman artefacts, columns, capitals, statuary, amphorae and so on.

Rabat is closely associated with St Paul and its landmark, the 17C **St Paul's Church**, is built above the **Grotto of St Paul**. Local legend has it that St Paul lived and preached here for several weeks, although other versions say he was imprisoned here. Whatever the truth, it has become a place of pilgrimage, and stone scraped from the grotto walls is supposed to have magical healing powers. Furthermore, so goes the story, no matter how much stone is scraped from the walls, the grotto never changes in size. In 1990 Pope John Paul II came here to pray.

Below the streets of Rabat lies a huge complex of early Christian catacombs. Over 3km² have been discovered so far, but there are probably many more. Their standard features, all hewn out of the stone, are the tombs which resemble shallow baths (all bodies have been removed), canopies over the tombs, and the characteristic *agape* circular 'tables', where mourning relatives would eat and drink in ritual remembrance of the deceased. There are two catacombs open to the public, both on St Agatha's Street. In **St Paul's Catacombs★★** you are left to do your own exploring, with only a scanty guide map (on sale) and very little light, which may be fun for fearless teenagers but is a little eerie for most visitors.

Ancient colourful frescoes decorate St Agatha's Catacombs.

Of far more interest are **St Agatha's Catacombs★★**, dedicated to the Sicilian saint who sought sanctuary from persecution here (though she was later martyred in Sicily). The highlight is the wonderful coloured **frescoes** which date from before the Arab invasion up to the 15C. Sadly, the earliest were (literally) defaced by the Muslims. An informative guided tour runs every 30 minutes.

Ta'Qali

On the road from Mdina to Valletta, old Second World War Nissen huts on a disused airfield are the rather cheerless setting for the **Ta'Qali Craft Centre**. A standard stopping-off place for coach tours, you can see weavers, carpenters, blacksmiths, potters, glass-blowers and lace-makers at work, and can buy their goods at below souvenir shop prices.

Glass-blowers need a good pair of lungs to shape Mdina glass, Ta'Qali Craft Centre.

THE CENTRE OF THE ISLAND

The Three Villages

The Three Villages, comprising Attard, Balzan and Lija (pronounced lee-yah), belie their sobriquet with little, if any resemblance to traditional villages. Perhaps this is a marketing exercise by local estate agents, as some of Malta's most desirable residences are to be found here. The most popular spot for visitors is **San Anton Gardens★**, nominally at Attard, though the gardens actually divide the three villages. The gardens are not large, but their lush, exotic greenery provides a welcome shady retreat from the burning summer sun. The small zoo and famous resident camel have gone, but the aviaries remain. The handsome residence in the grounds, **San Anton Palace**, was built in 1625 as a country retreat for a Grand Master. It was subsequently a home of the British Governor and is now the official residence of the President of Malta. It is not open to the public. Attard's other claim to fame is the **Church of St Mary★**, built in 1616 and probably the finest Renaissance building in Malta. Its architect, Tomasso Dingli, was only 22 years old when he designed it.

If you are on Malta around the first week of August don't miss the *festa* (*see* p.92) at Lija; it is one of the best on the island, and includes a spectacular fireworks display.

Luxuriant palms shade fountains and pots of vibrant flowers in San Anton Gardens, Attard.

Mosta

Mosta is famous for the great dome of its Church of St Mary, better known simply as **Mosta Dome★★**. Built between 1833 and 1860, the church's crowning glory measures 37m (122ft) in diameter. It is claimed to be the third largest unsupported church dome in Europe after St Peter's, Rome and St Sophia, Istanbul. One of Malta's landmarks, it is a marvellous sight from within and without. It also has a tale to tell. During the Second World War a bomb dropped straight through the church while it was full. Fortunately it failed to explode and so another Maltese miracle was born. You can see a replica of the bomb in the church.

Mosta Dome – this hugely impressive edifice took 27 years to construct and dwarfs the surrounding town.

Naxxar

Naxxar (pronounced Nash-ar) is one of the oldest settlements on the island, though these days it almost merges with Mosta. It is famous for hosting Malta's annual **International Fair** in July (*see* p.94). At any time of year it is worth a visit to look inside the recently opened **Palazzo Parisio★**, a beautiful 19C stately home with some of Malta's finest formal gardens (open Tue, Thur, Fri 9am-1pm).

THE NORTH

The north of the island is dominated by the two large holidays areas of Buġibba/ St Paul's Bay and Mellieħa Bay, which bite huge chunks from the north-eastern part of the coastline. Here, sandy bays nestle between rugged headlands and cliffs. The most appealing beaches, however, are on the west side, where development is relatively small scale. Compared to the rest of the island there is less of historical interest in the north, though it does contain some important sites.

Buġibba and St Paul's Bay (Il Bajja ta'San Pawl il-Baħar)
Despite being one of the island's most popular holiday spots, there is little evidence of traditional Maltese life in **Buġibba** (pronounced boo-jeeba). It is rather a tourist village which was created in the 1980s to meet a demand for budget package holidays. Its faceless tower block apartments and hotels, pubs, bars and fast-food outlets could be virtually anywhere in the Mediterranean. Its neighbour, **Qawra** (pronounced oar-a), occupies the other side of the peninsula, overlooking Salina Bay, and while being aimed slightly more upmarket, is every bit as anonymous. Neither resort possesses a beach, though

swimming and watersports are possible off
the Buġibba promenade.

Boat trips depart from Buġibba on
itineraries including a tour around St Paul's
Bay. In the bay is **St Paul's Island** (Gżejjer
ta'San Pawl), the spot where by tradition the
Apostle was shipwrecked in AD 60 (*see* p.9).

Captain Morgan's Underwater Safaris also
run out of Buġibba, and while there is
undoubted novelty value to sitting below the
waterline in a special glass-bottomed
observation deck, there is little marine life
to see (bookings from Captain Morgan
Cruises, Dolphin Court, Tigné Seafront,
Sliema ☎ **343 373**; *see* p.106).

In contrast to Buġibba the adjacent
settlement of **St Paul's Bay** (Il Bajja ta'San
Pawl il-Bahar) is a real Maltese community,
though it too is heavily overbuilt. Its most
attractive feature is the bay itself, with the
brightly painted *luzzus* bobbing in the old

*Built with the
tourist in mind,
Buġibba offers the
full range of
watersports off its
rocky coastline.*

harbour. You can enjoy its views from the Gillieru restaurant. The only sight of historical note is the restored **Wignacourt Tower**, built by Grand Master Alof de Wignacourt in 1610.

As you head north from St Paul's Bay you can't help but notice the brooding, castle-like **Selmun Palace**, set high above the bay, appearing and disappearing with every twist of the road. Built in the 18C as a fortified country house, it has recently been restored to create a French restaurant. Even if you're not dining here it's worth the short detour to admire it at close quarters. An annexe has been built at the rear of the Palace to house the Grand Hotel Mercure Selmun Palace.

Next to the small roundabout which turns off to Selmun you will notice a primitive small round hut, known as a *girna*, dating from the Bronze Age. On the other side of the road is the Belleview Bakery – great for fresh-from-the-oven sweet and savoury snacks.

A statue of St Paul dominates the uninhabited St Paul's Island.

Mellieħa Bay (Il Bajja tal-Mellieħa)

Mellieħa Bay has the largest sandy beach in the archipelago. This long, clean, golden arc (also known as Għadira Beach) is a great place to relax off-peak, but beware summer weekends when it gets desperately overcrowded. All the usual watersports are on offer in the bay. Huge traffic jams ensue and there isn't a parking place for miles along the roadside.

Impressively set high on a very steep hill overlooking the hoards below is the town of **Mellieħa**, a pleasant, largely unaffected place, with a fine church, the **Nativity of Our Lady**. Below the church is a chapel cut from the rocks, thought to date from the Early Christian period. The fresco of the Virgin Mary is a place of pilgrimage, visited in 1990 by Pope John Paul II.

Marfa Ridge

At the northernmost part of the island is the

Bright parasols dot Mellieħa Bay as it awaits the throngs of locals and tourists attracted by the wide, sandy beach.

little-visited Marfa Ridge, a hammerhead-shaped peninsula which appears to have been tacked on as an afterthought. Carry on up the main road past Mellieħa Bay, enjoying the **views**, and turn very sharp left at the crossroads up a horribly steep road to the Red Tower. Look down to your left for a bird's-eye-view of the **Għadira Nature Reserve**, one of the very few places on the island where birds may settle in safety, away from the guns of Malta's voracious hunting fraternity.

The **Red Tower**, almost identical in shape to the Selmun Palace, was built in 1649 by the Knights of St John as a lookout tower to warn of pirates and Turks. It now looks rather forlorn and has lost nearly all of its red paint, but it is open to the public. The westernmost tip of the island is just a little further along this road, with wonderful sea **views**.

Head straight back across the main road to the northern section of the Marfa Ridge road. Off here is signposted **Ramla Bay** (Ramla tat-Torri) and **Armier Bay** (Il Bajja ta' l-Armier), each of which has a small pleasant sandy beach and some basic seaside facilities. There is watersports equipment for hire at the Ramla Bay Hotel. Both beaches are busy in summer but nonetheless may provide a quieter alternative to Mellieħa Bay at peak periods. The road continues to the very cliff top, where there is a Madonna statue. This is popular hiking country; you can head downhill and make a circuit right around the northern half of Marfa Ridge.

The main road from Armier Bay leads to **Cirkewwa**, where there is another good sandy, but much oversubscribed, beach. The ferry for Gozo departs from closeby.

West Coast Beaches

At Anchor Bay on the western side of the island is the incongruous yet highly popular **Popeye Village**. Yes, right here in Malta, at the wonderfully ramshackle Newfoundland-style fishing village of Sweethaven, you can see where Popeye socked it to Bluto and swept Olive Oyl off her feet! Built in 1980 for *Popeye* the movie, starring Robin Williams, it has stayed the course considerably longer than the memory of the actual film. It's like wandering around a very picturesque ghost town and is extremely photogenic. There's even a small beach and other children's amusements to entice you to spend longer here.

Something a little different – at Popeye Village the set from the film has become an attraction in itself.

The most picturesque route to Għajn Tuffieħa (pronounced ein-tuff-ee-ah; it means 'eye of the apple') is from the north via Manikata, though most visitors simply cut across the island from St Paul's Bay. Here you will find two of the island's best sandy beaches. **Golden Bay** (Ir-Ramla tal-Mixquqa) is well named, a very popular soft sandy cove with most watersports and other beach facilities. It is overlooked by the Golden Sands and another small hotel, but otherwise is largely unspoiled. It does get very crowded in high season, however. A popular trip from here is a horse trek to Popeye Village. The adjacent sandy crescent of **Għajn Tuffieħa Bay★** (Ir-Ramla ta'Għajn Tuffieħa) is even more attractive, with dramatic rock formations. It is unspoiled by hotel developments though there are pedaloes and umbrellas for hire.

A short but quite strenuous walk away to the south is **Għnejna Bay** (Il-Bajja tal-Għnejna, pronounced je-nay-na). Its limited shingle-sand beach is augmented by large flat rocks which make ideal sunbathing beds. Local colour is provided by islanders' holiday homes and caves which the fishermen use as boathouses. You can also drive to Għnejna from the direction of Mġarr.

Historic Sites

Although not as prolific as the south, the north of the island boasts some of Malta's oldest archaeological sites. The **Skorba temple complex**, just outside Żebbiegħ, is the island's earliest Neolithic settlement, where two temples and several houses have been revealed in excavations. There are two similar temples at **Ta'Ħaġrat**, near Mġarr, but neither site is officially open to the public.

Mysteries in Stone

The temples at **Skorba** and **Mġarr** (Ta'Ħaġrat) on Malta, and **Ġgantija**★★ on Gozo are the oldest free-standing structures in the world, dating from around 3250 BC – older than both the pyramids of Egypt and Stonehenge in Britain.

As at other massive Neolithic sites, one of the questions always asked by visitors is, 'How were the stones transported to the site and moved into position?' A system of rollers and levers is the most likely explanation. It is thought that some of the huge blocks were transported

on stone spheres found buried in some of the temples, but archaeologists are still puzzled as to how some of the massive temple stones, weighing many tonnes, were erected upright. Even the locals have no idea, taking refuge in legends, such as that of the female giant who carried the great blocks of Ġgantija to the temple site from Ta'Cenc, nearly 4km (2.5 miles) away.

Many visitors come away from Malta's temple remains baffled simply because there are no interpretation facilities on site. It's a good idea to visit the island's archaeological museums first to try to get a background history, but even then it's best to visit the temples with a knowledgeable guide. If you're not with a group ask the site custodian to take you around.

Even more enigmatic than the temples are the so-called **Cart Ruts at Clapham Junction** (humorously named after the busiest railway station in Britain) near Buskett Gardens. There are other less well-known examples on Gozo. Comprising a series of parallel stone grooves in the rock surface, they are thought to have been some sort of early tramlines, designed to facilitate the movement of sledges or wheeled vehicles. If this was the case, then the tracks that lead straight over the cliff top may be the earliest evidence of fly-tipping!

Above: The curious Cart Ruts at Clapham Junction, near Rabat.
Left: Older than the pyramids, the Ġgantija temples, Gozo.

GOZO★

They say that if you want to see what Malta looked like 40 years ago then go to Gozo. Its topography and character is, unsurprisingly, similar to Malta, but this is a much more rural, peaceful place. Industry, large-scale building development and mass tourism are absent and the pace of life is correspondingly much slower than on the 'big island'. It is also greener, with wooded, fertile valleys which give Gozo a more gentle feel.

Gozo is small, measuring just 15km by 7km (roughly 9 miles by 4 miles), but many of its roads radiate out from the central town of Victoria like the spokes of a wheel, and to tour the island involves a fair amount of backtracking.

Map of Gozo.

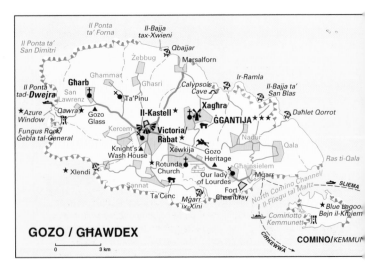

The most popular means of arrival is via the ferry, which departs from Cirkewwa at Malta's north-easternmost point. It takes vehicles and foot passengers and makes the crossing in around 30 minutes. (Until recently there was another service from Pietà Creek, near Valletta, but that is now for cargo only.) A passenger-only hovermarine service also operates from Sliema to Gozo in the summer, and takes about 25 minutes.

Another option is to take the 10-minute helicopter ride from Malta's Luqa airport, touching down at Xewkija. This is how the majority of international travellers who are staying on Gozo for the duration of their holiday arrive, stepping straight from plane to helicopter (for reservations contact Air Malta offices world-wide, Gozo Heliport ☎ 557 905/561 301, or Air Malta ☎ 662 211/6).

First impressions

Most visitors' first sight of Gozo is **Mġarr** (pronounced im-jar), an attractive sheltered fishing and commercial port with a large complement of brightly painted *luzzus* and other colourful fishing boats at anchor alongside yachts, international cargo vessels and, of course, a ferry or two, waiting to shuttle back to Malta. Above it all, high on the cliff, is the neo-Gothic church of **Our Lady of Lourdes**.

Aside from a tourist information office there's nothing else to detain visitors, who generally head straight for the capital, Victoria (also known as Rabat). At the summit of the hill, most visitors rush past **Fort Chambray** without even seeing it. It was planned to be a fortress town and began construction in the early 1700s, but the

project was never realised. There is no
public access at present, though it may be
turned into a holiday village in the near
future.

Drive along the main road for around five
minutes and on the right-hand side is **Gozo
Heritage**, a 'welcome-to-Gozo' style
attraction with a series of tableaux and
audio-visual effects giving a potted history of
the island (open Mon-Sat 9am-5.15pm). You
would do better to wait until Victoria's Gozo
Experience, however. There's a shop, too,
selling typical Gozitan goods, which you can
look at without paying admission.

After another kilometre turn right to
Xewkija (pronounced show-key-ya), where
the pride and joy of this small village-town is
its **Rotunda Church★**. It is said to have the
fourth largest dome in Europe, just a little
smaller than the famous dome of Mosta.

*The Rotunda
Church evokes a
somnolent
atmosphere over
the deserted streets
of Xewkija.*

Victoria★ (Rabat)

Victoria took its name from the reigning British monarch in 1897, celebrating the year of Queen Victoria's diamond jubilee. Locals prefer the original Arab name, Rabat, and both names are still used, which can cause some confusion with the town of Rabat on Malta.

A little-visited spot is **Rundle Gardens**, just on the left before the centre of town. Like Malta, Gozo has few woods or gardens so any green space with a splash of colour is worth knowing about.

The central square is **Pjazza d'Independenza** (Independence Square), also known as It-Tokk meaning 'the meeting place'. Aside from the low-key bustle of the daily morning market, it is a quiet, shady spot where old men sit around on benches and the pace of life is relaxed. Look in at the atmospheric Central Coffee House Sopos, which is a cross between an old-fashioned café and a British pub.

Just off the square is Castle Hill, on the corner of which is the **Gozo 360°**. This is an audio-visual theatre show, very much in the mould of the successful Malta Experience, and offers a good introduction to the island (open Mon-Sat 10.30am-4.30pm; Sun 10am-1.30pm).

The Citadel★ (Il-Kastell)

Castle Hill leads to the Citadel, the fortified heart of the island to which Gozo's citizens would retreat at times of danger. It's a pleasant, well restored place, perhaps a little over-restored, and lacking the atmosphere of Malta's other fortified towns. Built around 1600, long after the Great Siege, it has never seen any serious action. The centrepiece is the **Cathedral★**, designed by the Maltese architect Lorenzo Gafà, and a fine example of Maltese vernacular Baroque. Like St John's Co-Cathedral on Malta, it is plain on the outside but ornate within. This cathedral was allocated far fewer funds than St John's however, and there was not enough even to cap it with a real dome, hence the clever *trompe l'oeil* ceiling painting, by Italian Antonio Manuele, which dates from the 1730s. It has, no doubt, fooled more than a few visitors.

The finest aspect of the Citadel is its far-reaching **views★**. Take a stroll around its walls and you can see most of the island. The Citadel includes five small museum collections which you will stumble upon as you walk around – it's a very small place. The charming **Folklore Museum** is the best, with well-arranged displays representing Gozitan life and housed in three restored medieval buildings. The **Archaeological Museum** is also worth a visit, not only for its setting within a 17C *palazzo*, but for the finds from the temples at Ggantija, and Punic, Greek and Roman exhibits. Behind the Cathedral is the **Cathedral Museum**, with the usual array of vestments, manuscripts and silverware. More unusual is the 19C ceremonial carriage of the Bishop of Gozo. Two museums in Quarters Street are the **Knights' Armoury**, where weaponry is displayed in the former British barracks, and the **Natural History Museum**, cataloguing the island's flora, fauna and geology.

Go back down Castle Hill, across the main road, through the narrow streets and tucked away on its own small square you will find Victoria's second major church, **St George's Basilica**, built in 1673. Its sumptuous

Baroque gilded interior comes as quite a
surprise and has earned it the nickname of
'the Golden Basilica'. The bronze altar
canopy is styled on Bernini's in St Peter's,
Rome.

Ta'Pinu and Għarb★

Two kilometres (1 mile) west of Victoria
turn right to find Malta's holiest shrine, the
Basilica of Ta'Pinu. Heavenly voices were
supposedly heard in the previous church on
this site in the late 19C. Then over the
following decades several miraculous cures
occurred in the area and Gozo escaped a
plague that struck Malta. In 1920 the
present neo-Romanesque church was built.
Subsequently elevated to Basilica status by
the Pope, it is an important place of
pilgrimage for Maltese and Gozitans.

*Peaceful, rural
scenes are typical
of Gozo.*

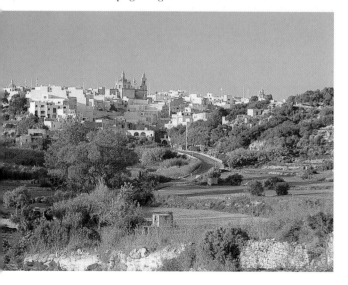

Continuing west, just off the main road, **Għarb★** is Gozo's most attractive village. At its entrance is **Gozo Glass** where you can see craftsmen at work. In the central square is the superb typically Maltese Baroque golden sandstone **Church of the Immaculate Conception**, with its unusual concave façade. As a visual counterpoint on the square are the old British Empire trappings of a red telephone box and a blue police lamp. Don't miss a visit to the excellent **Għarb Folklore Museum**, set in a beautiful 18C stone house around a peaceful courtyard. All manner of fascinating commercial and domestic bygones are displayed in its warren of 28 tiny rooms, and if you are lucky an old

The Basilica of Ta'Pinu has a curious history of celestial voices and miraculous happenings.

man will be playing an accordion to make the atmosphere even more mellow (closed Sun pm).

Dwejra Point (Il Ponta tad-Dwejra)

The road continues through San Lawrenz to Dwejra Point (pronounced d'way-rah). The spectacular natural rock arch which dominates this beauty spot is known, for obvious reasons, as the **Azure Window★** (Tieqa Zerqa) and is one of Gozo's most photographed features. Sunset here is a spectacular sight and many tours are specially timed for this event. Walk over the small hill behind the solitary refreshments hut and you will find the fancifully named **Inland Sea★** (Il Qawra). From this small lagoon you can take a boat ride through another natural arch out to the sea proper.

The small bay behind you, as you face the Azure Window, is famous for the enigmatically titled **Fungus Rock** (Ġebla tal-General). This green-topped rocky outcrop was once harvested by the Knights of St John for *'fungus Gaulitanus'*, an unusual vegetation which was thought to cure

Shades of blue merge from deep indigo to turquoise; shadow and sunlight play on the surface of the water – the sea at its most beautiful.

The natural arch of the Azure Window provides the frame for stunning views and sunsets.

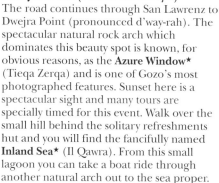

A deep fissure feeds the Inland Sea from the tumultuous coastal waters, yet it remains tranquil – perfect for bathing.

dysentry and to stop haemorrhaging. The Knights built the adjacent **Qawra Tower** to guard this prized possession; the penalty for stealing it was death. It has since been shown that the plant is actually of no medicinal value, nor is it even a fungus.

The South Coast

The road descends steeply to the south coast, following an attractive lush river valley. Just as you are leaving the suburbs of Victoria, at Fontana, is the 17C **Knight's Wash House**, a small construction built over a spring.

Xlendi★ (pronounced shlen-dee) is a charming small resort set at the head of a deep, calm inlet. It has a tiny promenade

It can take a while to get around in Gozo, but no one minds the leisurely pace.

with a handful of hotels and bars, and a pocket handkerchief-sized beach which is hopelessly overcrowded in the summer. Its quiet water is an excellent spot for swimming and snorkelling, and diving expeditions also depart from here.

Rough minor roads continue along the coastline east to the agricultural village of Sannat where elderly ladies can be seen sitting outside their houses making the beautiful lace the island is noted for. Beyond the village is **Ta'Cenc**, famous for its eponymous luxury hotel, imposing cliffs, and a smattering of prehistoric remains, including mysterious cart ruts, similar to those on Malta, and prehistoric dolmens. Nearby is the narrow rocky cove of **Mġarr-ix-Xini**, where locals enjoy a swim.

The North Coast

Gozo's main holiday resort is **Marsalforn** which sits in a sheltered harbour. By Gozo standards it is large and overdeveloped, though it is still plied by traditional fishing boats. There is a small pebble-and-sand beach, but swimming is best off its rocky ledges. There are two quieter rocky bays for

Make the most of your time on the golden sandy beach of Ramla Bay, but beware of strong currents.

swimming immediately to the west at Qbajjar and Zwieni.

The road east leads to **Calypso's Cave**. By legend, Gozo is known as the island of Calypso, the sea siren who lured Odysseus and held him for seven years in her cave. Owing to a rock fall which blocked the main cave you can now only enter what is effectively a rocky cleft (claustrophobes beware!). Various 'attendants' will show you the entrance and accompany you a short way inside with a torch. If the cave is nothing special, it's still worth coming up here just for the view down to **Ramla Bay** (Ir-Ramla) which is Gozo's best beach. In fact, this is the island's only real soft sandy beach and is consequently very popular, though there is no development as yet to mar its natural beauty. There are refreshments, watersports and sunshades for hire, but beware when swimming as notices warn of dangerous currents and reefs.

If Ramla Bay is too busy, try the charming sandy cove of **San Blas**, just a little way to the east as the crow flies, but a long loop via Nadur by car. You will have to park your car a little distance away then walk down the steep narrow track, but it is well worth the effort. Take a picnic.

There is one more option for getting away from it all, east at **Daħlet Qorrot**. Like San Blas, this too is an attractive cove reached by a steep walk and favoured by locals. There is no sand here though.

Ġgantija★★★ and Xagħra

The **Ġgantija Temples★★★** (pronounced jee-gan-tee-ya) are as old as any man-made thing in the Maltese archipelago. The name derives from the temples' giant size; some of the stones are up to 6m (20ft) tall and weigh many tonnes. Legend has it that a female giant carried the blocks from Ta'Cenc on her head. Ġgantija is the best preserved of Malta's Neolithic remains, and comprises two temples with libation holes, blocks with spiral decorations, an oracle hole and a recess for washing feet. It is possible to walk right into the temples, but you will need a guide to make sense of it all.

Very close to Ġgantija, on the edge of the town of Xagħra (pronounced shuh-ra) is **Ta'Kola Windmill Museum★**, a beautifully restored flour mill, built in 1725. You can see the miller's living quarters, the blacksmith's shop and various other rural Gozitan memorabilia.

Xagħra has a fine central square with a splendid church, the anachronistically named Coronation Stores, and good places to eat and drink. Just off the square are two privately owned caves and a small toy museum. Both **Xerri's Grotto** (pronounced sherry's) and the smaller **Ninu's Cave** are full of curiously shaped stalactites and stalagmites. **Pomskizillious Toy Museum** was inspired by Edward Lear, the name itself a typically nonsensical adjective that Lear attributed to the island of Gozo – 'pomskizillious and gromphiberous, being as no words can describe its magnificence'. There's a wax model of Lear, ancient automata, and toys that go back over 150 years.

COMINO

The tiny island of Comino, measuring just 2.5 km^2 (1sq mile), is only 1km (0.6 miles) away from Gozo at its nearest point and 4km (2.5 miles) from Cirkewwa on Malta. Its main attraction is its **Blue Lagoon★** (Bejn il-Kmiemen), a small strait that divides Comino from the even tinier islet of Cominotto. Certainly the name is not

Striking, iridescent, aquamarine – the Blue Lagoon couldn't be more inviting.

hyperbole. The waters are the most glorious shades of aquamarine and a steady trickle of pleasure boats queue to deposit divers, snorkellers and swimmers into this liquid blue. They come from Mġarr on Gozo, and from Buġibba and Sliema on Malta.

Comino has two unobtrusive hotels, the Comino, and its sister, Club Nautico, which leads diving expeditions and hires out other watersports equipment. The Comino has a wonderfully located swimming pool and a beautiful private small beach at San Niklaw Bay. Aside from this and a 17C Knights' **lookout tower**, Comino is virtually empty (it is said just five people live here permanently). Best of all for those in search of peace and quiet, there is not a single motor vehicle to disturb the tranquillity.

It is obvious why Hotel Comino, San Niklaw Bay, is so sought after – all you have to decide is which aquatic sanctuary you fancy.

WEATHER

Malta enjoys the hot summers and mild winters of a typical Mediterranean climate. Even between October and March there is an average of 6 hours of sunshine per day, and temperatures of around 14°C (57°F). During the peak summer months of July and August it reaches a blistering 30-35°C (86-95°F). Sea breezes relieve the heat, but not so the hot *sirocco* which brings hot air from the Sahara.

Historically, October is by far the wettest month, with a rainfall of around 120mm (almost 5in), but you should take an umbrella at any time between late September and March. Showers generally soon clear, however, to reveal cloudless blue skies. The best times to visit are May, June and early September.

CALENDAR OF EVENTS

The festa

In addition to the events listed below, between mid April and the end of September each town and village celebrates its particular patron saint's day feast or *festa*, with religious processions, decorated streets and illuminated churches, street food and drink and fireworks. *Festas* generally run from Wednesday through to Sunday. The tourist office may have details of what's on while you are in Malta, but with some 150 towns and villages each holding a *festa*, you are sure to catch one somewhere. Evening excursions are run by operators to some of the best *festa* fireworks displays.

February

10 February: Feast of St Paul's Shipwreck, in Valletta, celebrating the shipwreck and arrival of St Paul on the island in AD 60.
Mid-late February (week preceding Lent): Carnival in Malta may not take on the earth-shaking celebrations of Rio, or parts of Spain, but the colourful processions, floats, grotesque masks and exuberant open-air dancing competitions are a definite highlight of the Maltese calendar, for visitors and locals alike. The main celebrations are in Valletta.

March

31 March: Freedom Day, marking the final withdrawal of the British Army from Malta, begins with a morning service at the War Memorial in Floriana. In the afternoon traditional regatta boat races (with two and four oarsmen) are held in Grand Harbour. One of the best places to watch is from the bastions at Senglea Point.

March/April

Easter: On Good Friday, pageants which depict scenes from the Passion and death of Jesus are held at around 5pm in 14 different towns and villages. On Easter Sunday statues of 'The Risen Christ' are carried through the streets. In the Three Cities it is traditional for the statue bearers to run with the statue.

April

Around mid-April (third Sunday after Easter) – September: The *festa* season (see above) starts with the celebrations of St Publius at Floriana.

Life is a carnival in Valletta.

June

29 June: *Mnarja* (pronounced im-nar-yah), the feast of St Peter and St Paul. This is Malta's most important folklore event. Festivities commence on the evening before, with open-air folk singing and music at Buskett Gardens and continue until the early hours of the next day. Traditional Maltese dishes are served, with fried rabbit being the speciality of the evening. Festivities continue on the day of the 29th with band marches and an agricultural show. During the afternoon traditional bareback horse and donkey races are held at Rabat (Malta) and Victoria (Gozo).

Late June-July

Maltafest is the most important cultural event on the Maltese calendar, with a wide range of activities including orchestral concerts, recitals, a film festival, open-air theatre, ballet and jazz, provided by local and foreign artists.

July

1-15 July: The International Trade Fair is held in the grounds of the Palazzo Parisio at Naxxar.
End July: The Malta Jazz Festival attracts some of the finest jazz musicians in the world (Chick Corea, Al di Meola and the Crusaders have all performed in the past). The Farsons International Food and Beer Festival is held the following weekend in Ta'Xbiex, and provides more live entertainment to accompany the eating and drinking.

September

8 September: Our Lady of Victories commemorates not only the day when the Great Siege of 1565 was lifted, but also the capitulation of the French in 1800 and the end of the 1942 siege by the Axis powers. A regatta is held in Grand Harbour, Valletta, in the afternoon and festivities follow at Senglea, Naxxar and Mellieħa on Malta, and on Xagħra in Gozo.
20 September: Independence Day. A day of general celebrations throughout the island.

October

First weekend October: The Mdina Festival is a celebration of heritage and pageantry, folklore, music and dance.

December

13 December: Republic Day festivities include parades, fireworks and horse races at Marsa.

ACCOMMODATION

Much of Malta's present holiday accommodation was built in the 1970s and 1980s to attract the package holiday market. The result is a surfeit of mediocre-quality high-rise hotels and apartments. The main benefit for the visitor is, of course, price. Recently there has been a tendency to build a better class of 4- and 5-star hotels in a bid to move Malta's image more up-market.

On Gozo the situation is very different. The island has never been a mass-market destination and has developed a low-rise unobtrusive style of accommodation, as characterised by a good number of converted farmhouses. In comparison to Malta's numerous cheap and cheerful offerings, they can be quite expensive.

Hotels are rated from 5-star down to 1-star according to the service and facilities they offer. A rough guide to prices, per person per night, is as follows. Be aware, however, that on a package, particularly a late availability package, you need pay only a fraction of this rate:
3-star: Lm18-20
4-star: Lm20-55
5-star: Lm60-110

In general, **self-catering** accommodation is plentiful, especially around St Julian's, Qawra and Buġibba, and ranges from the basic one-room studios to large apartments in complexes offering a wide range of facilities. Prices are regulated by the Hotels and Catering Establishments Board, and a list of self-catering accommodation can be obtained from them at 280 Republic Street, Valletta, Malta, CMR 02, ☎ 220 132.

Holiday complexes are graded from first to third class. Those which are rated 'first class' approximate in standards and prices to 4-star hotels. There is a choice of **Aparthotels**, popular with families who may prefer self-catering accommodation. These are also graded from first to third class.

There is not a great tradition of **bed-and-breakfast** accommodation in Malta, although there is a range of **guest houses**, particularly in Sliema, and private rooms can be rented. Guest houses are also graded from first to third class and the local tourist office will be able to provide a list of these, together with all the other types of accommodation outlined above.

The Malta Tourist Office in your home country will be able to provide a list of tour companies who operate in Malta.

Contact the Malta Tourist Office, Malta House, 36-38 Piccadilly, London W1V 0PP ☎ (020) 7292 4900; Malta National Tourist Office, Empire State Building, 350 Fifth Ave, Suite 4412, New York 10118 ☎ (212) 695 9520.

Malta lists five official **youth hostels** and Gozo has one. Contact the Malta Youth Hostels Association, 182-3 Tower Road, Sliema, SLM10, Malta ☎ 344 345.

There are no official **camping** sites on the islands.

Recommendations

To call Malta from abroad, prefix the following numbers with ☎ 00 356.

Malta
Balzan

Corinthia Palace Hotel 5-stars (*De Paule Ave, San Anton* ☎ 440 301 fax 441 042) Situated in the centre of Malta, half-way between Valletta and Mdina, this hotel is set in landscaped gardens. It provides a wide range of facilities including high-quality accommodation and food, a swimming pool and terrace restaurant and the Athenaeum Health Spa, which offers individual programmes of treatments.
Corinthia Beach Resort includes the **Corinthia San**

Gorg Hotel 5-stars (☎ 374 114 fax 378 222) and the **Corinthia Marina Hotel** 4-stars (☎ 381 720 fax 381 708) Located in St George's Bay, next to St Julian's, this resort offers extensive facilities, with eight restaurants and five bars, including a Vinotheque & Cheese Bar, Tapas Bar, ice-cream parlour, and American-style bar and grill. There are large terraces and pools, a private lido, a thalassotherapy centre and indoor heated pool, and a nightclub.
Selmun/Mellieħa
Grand Hotel Mercure Selmun Palace 4-stars (*Selmun SPB 10* ☎ 521 040 fax 521 159; toll-free number for UK calls ☎ 181 283 4500, in New York ☎ 1 800 221 4542) Situated in the north of Malta, near St Paul's Bay. All rooms have balconies, some have sea views to Gozo and Comino while others overlook the large swimming pool, with the 18C Selmun Castle and St Paul's Bay in the background. The French restaurant, Le Chateau, is open for dinner only. Facilities include outdoor swimming pool (sea water), indoor pool with sauna, free transport to the small sandy beach of Selmun, theme evenings and buffets.
St Paul's Bay
Mistra Village Club First Class

(*Xemxija Hill, St Paul's Bay* ☎ **580 481** fax 582 941) Very attractive small holiday club comprising low-level apartments; popular with the 30-something crowd.

Valletta

Le Meridien Phoenicia 5-stars (*The Mall, Floriana* ☎ **225 241** fax 235 254) Set immediately outside Valletta's City Gate and surrounded by seven acres of landscaped gardens, this luxury hotel is ideal for a short winter break, particularly if you intend spending time in Valletta; popular with business types.

The Osborne Hotel 3-stars (*50 South Street, Valletta* ☎ **232 127/8** fax 232 120)

Marsamxett Harbour, Sliema.

Simple hotel situated just a stone's throw away from the ramparts. All rooms have air conditioning. The terrace, on the 6th floor, includes a tiny swimming pool. Bar and restaurant (buffet only for dinner).

Sliema

Fortina 4-stars (*Tigné Seafront* ☎ **342 976** fax 339 388) The best situated hotel on the island, with magnificent views across to Valletta and conveniently close to Sliema and Valletta. An all-inclusive tariff at very reasonable rates.

Gozo
Mġarr

L-Imgarr Hotel 5-stars (*Mgarr GSM 104, Gozo* ☎ **560 455/6/7** fax 557 589) Standing above

Mġarr harbour, the L-Imgarr Hotel offers gorgeous views of the bay, together with very comfortable suite-style bedrooms, two swimming pools, and a very good restaurant which serves mostly Italian-style dishes in a luxurious setting and with first-class service.

Sannat

Ta'Cenc 5-stars (*Sannat, Gozo* ☎ **556 819** fax 558 199) A quiet luxury hideaway of bungalows set around two swimming pools and landscaped grounds, with a rocky cove for swimming. The relaxed atmosphere, food and service are all first class.

Xlendi

St Patrick's Hotel 4-stars (*Xlendi, VCT 115, Gozo* ☎ **562 951/2** fax 556 598) Located in front of Xlendi beach; 48 rooms, some with balcony offering sea views (those with internal views onto the patio may be a little dark). There is a tiny swimming pool on the 6th floor terrace, a beach restaurant and bar.

Xagħra

Cornucopia 4-stars (*10 Gnien Imrik St* ☎ **556 486** fax 552 910) This small, low-rise family-run converted farmhouse features accommodation in rustic rooms with luxury facilities. (The Cornucopia also offers a selection of farmhouses to rent in neighbouring villages, and guests can use the hotel facilities.)

FOOD AND DRINK

Eating out in Malta is rarely a gourmet event, but there is a wide range of restaurants to suit all tastes and pockets. Valletta features a handful of fine restaurants and in the resorts of Sliema, St Julian's and St George's Bay you will find food from all over the world. There are also plenty of bland, international-style menus to choose from. Often the only thing that is missing is a traditional Maltese restaurant. As a general rule, if you are stuck for a decision look for a pizzeria or an Italian-run establishment as these invariably produce the best value for money.

Maltese cuisine

True Maltese restaurants are rare and even Maltese dishes are not common, particularly in tourist areas, but they are worth seeking out.

As you would expect on an island, **fish** is abundant. Typical fish dishes are *aljotta* (a fish soup); *accjola* (amberjack); *cerna* (grouper) *espadon, pixxispad* or *pesce espada* (all names for swordfish); and *lampuki* (dorado), in season from September to November. Try the swordfish Maltese-style, smothered in a robust sauce of tomatoes and capers. Another speciality is *lampuki* served in a pie, *torta tal-lampuki*, mixed with tomatoes, onions, olives, and various other vegetables. Other unusual fish names you may come across are *dott* (stone bass), *dentici* (sea bream) and *sargu* (white bream).

You won't find many cows grazing in the fields in Malta, but *bragjoli* (a type of beef olive) is definitely worth a try. The favourite **meat** dish is *fenek* (rabbit). This may be served *bizzalza* (casseroled) or fried. Rabbit is the Maltese celebration dish and a traditional *fenkata* evening usually comprises a menu of spaghetti with rabbit sauce, rabbit, then nuts and figs. For the average visitor, rabbit is fiddly and bony but very tasty.

Maltese sausages, which are of the British link variety (as opposed to the continental slicing style) are delicious, often flavoured with lemon and herbs.

Cheese and pasta dishes
reflect the Italian influence. The two favourites are: *timpana*, baked macaroni with meat, eggs and cheese topped with flaky pastry; and *ross fil-forn*, a savoury rice dish baked with eggs, tomatoes, saffron and meat. You may also find these sold in the street in square, silver-tray containers as take-away snack meals. Another Maltese dish with an obvious Italian connection is *ravjul* (pronounced rav-yul), ravioli filled with cheese. A very different sort of typically Maltese cheese dish is *gbejniet* (or *gbejna*), a round of peppered goats' cheese. It is usually served with salad as a starter.

Snacks and sweet things
It's easy to find typical Maltese snacks, both in cafés or sold in the street. The ubiquitous lunchtime filler is *hobz bizet*, (or *hobz biz-zejt*), which translates as 'bread with oil'. This is a delicious typically Mediterranean snack of bread smeared with a paste of tomatoes, garlic, capers and olive oil, then filled with tuna, olives and salad. It may also be served toasted (like the Italian *bruschetta*) as a starter in restaurants. Some places advertise *hobz bizet* as 'Maltese Bread'. A favourite morning snack is a *pastizzi rikotta* (flaky ricotta cheese envelope) or a *qassatat* (pronounced ass-er-tat), a round flaky or shortcrust pie filled with either cheese or yellow mashed marrowfat peas. The latter is sometimes referred to as a *pizelli*. These are sold fresh from the oven and are best eaten warm. If you are passing a bakery early in the morning, do pop in to see what's cooking. If the wind is blowing your way then you probably won't be able to resist

a visit. Another tempting aroma that will linger long in the nostrils is the smell of *mqarets*, deep fried date pastries, always on sale by the main gate to Valletta.

Like the Italians, the Maltese have a sweet tooth and it's always a treat to pop into a *pasticeria* to have a coffee and to choose from the mouth-watering display of sweet (and often savoury) pastries and other confections on offer. Some *pasticerrias* are like an Aladdin's Cave, brimming full of exquisitely pre-packaged cakes, sweets, chocolates, snacks and just about every form of fattening comestible known to man.

A table with a view to complement the Mediterranean-style seafood.

Nougat is very popular, and at festival times nougat street-stands are a common sight.

Drinks

The Maltese have inherited coffee from the Italians and tea from the British, so they are equally at home with either, though the coffee is nearly always a better bet.

The British, too, are largely responsible for at least one of the island's two ubiquitous **beer** brands. Pale ale may have long disappeared from mainstream British drinking, but the dark, cold, fizzy, Hopleaf Pale Ale is still a best-seller in Malta. Cisk Lager (pronounced chisk) is its companion brew. A pleasant lightly alcoholic drink in the heat of day is Farson's Shandy, another traditional British drink, blending beer and lemonade.

Maltese wines have come on in leaps and bounds in recent years, and good quality wines by Marsovin, the local standard bearer, are excellent, as are the Marnisi, Cheval Franc and Antonin Blanc, while the Verdala Bianco Secco and Rose are also good. The cellars of Marsovin can be visited ☎ 699 62310/824 918. Gozo makes its own wines – gutsy and with a kick, if you can find a bottle.

The national soft drink is Kinnie, a refreshing cola-style

beverage, flavoured with bitter oranges and aromatic herbs. After dinner try the national liqueur, Tamaki, derived from carob pods.

Recommendations

Eating out is generally inexpensive by northern European standards. For a three-course meal, per person without wine, you can expect to pay the following:
Inexpensive: under Lm5
Moderate: Lm5-8
Expensive: over Lm8

Malta
Sliema
Mangal (moderate to expensive) *Tigné Seafront* ☎ **341 046** Highly-rated Turkish restaurant. In summer book for the terrace, which enjoys magnificent views to Valletta (open for dinner only; closed on Sundays).
La Cuccagna (inexpensive) *47 Amery Street, off Tower Road* ☎ **346 703** Great little pizzeria, usually packed to the gills with locals. Very friendly; booking essential.
Ta'Kolina (moderate) *151 Tower Road* ☎ **335 106** Small and friendly, popular with tourists and locals – *the* place to try Maltese specialities.

Valletta
Trattoria da Pippo *136 Melita Street* ☎ **248 029** Picturesque little restaurant where Maltese people like to go for lunch. Mainly fish (swordfish and tuna) but also some Maltese dishes (closed evenings and on Sundays).
Bologna (expensive) *59 Republic Street* ☎ **246 149** Renowned Italian restaurant, also serving Maltese specialities.
Giannini (expensive) *23 Triq il-Mithna (Windmill St)* ☎ **237 121** One of Valletta's best Italian restaurants, with great views over Marsamxett Harbour.
Roof Top Restaurant, Castille Hotel ☎ **243 677** Enjoying an unbeatable view over Grand Harbour, with simple dining on the open-air terrace.
The Phoenix Restaurant, Hotel Phoenicia Even if you are not staying at this grand hotel, try the creative menu of its restaurant. Good French-style cuisine with a touch of Maltese flavour in some of the *à la carte* dishes; served in a comfortable setting, with open-air terrace for those who enjoy the fresh air, and good views of the Grand Harbour. Extensive wine list.
The Carriage (expensive) *Valletta Buildings, South Street* ☎ **247 828** High class restaurant situated right at the top of the building, with terrace offering splendid views over the ancient town and Marsamxett

harbour. Elegant setting, excellent international cuisine and service. (Lunch Monday to Friday, dinner Friday and Saturday.)

Mdina
The Medina Restaurant (expensive) *7 Holy Cross Street* ☎ **454 004** Quiet and romantic, tucked away in a side street in a typical old Mdina house. International cuisine (open for dinner only; closed on Sundays).

Bacchus *Triq Inguanez* ☎ **454 981** Installed in an old vaulted setting, with natural stone walls adorned with barrels, this is refreshingly cool when it's hot outside. Try one of their Maltese specialities, such as *Tender Maltese Escargot*, served with an original garlic paste dip (open for lunch and dinner).

Mosta
Ta'Marija *Triq Constitution* ☎ **434 444** Situated in the main street of Mosta, very near to Mosta Dom, this large restaurant is in a converted farmhouse, with the bar at the entrance featuring a galleon. Renowned for its authentic Maltese cuisine, including a wide range of local fish dishes (grilled swordfish, tuna served with piquant sauce) and meat dishes (try fried rabbit or *Bragioli*). Also serves continen-

tal-style dishes, and often has music and dancing at weekends (open daily for lunch and dinner).

Mellieħa
The Arches (expensive) *113 Main Street* ☎ **573 436** Very elegant spot serving excellent international cuisine.

St Julian's
Barracuda (expensive) *Triq il-Kbira* ☎ **331 817** At the corner between St Julian's Bay and Balluta Bay, and next to the Piccolo Padre, this restaurant enjoys a wonderful situation. Very good food (mainly fish with Italian flavours) and high-class service (reservation recommended).

Caffe Raffael (inexpensive) *Spinola Bay* ☎ **332 000** A good spot in St Julian's for a snack, on an open-air terrace at the head of the picturesque Spinola Bay. The Italian food, mostly pizzas and pasta, is good too.

San Giuliano Restaurant *Spinola Bay* ☎ **332 000** Under the same management as Caffe Raffael, next door. The restaurant is on an open-air terrace overlooking the bay, on the first floor (no lift, so not recommended for disabled people). Italian cuisine, fresh fish, antipasti and pasta dishes; good selection of Italian and Maltese wines.

Piccolo Padre (inexpensive) *195 Main St, Balluta Bay* ☎ 344 875 Lively popular basement of a rustic 18C house in a marvellous position overlooking the bay. Good pizzas and pastas.

Marsaxlokk

Pisces ☎ 684 956 Facing the harbour front, with good views of the bay and the colourful *luzzus*; mainly fresh fish, including octopus, lobster and squid.

Ta'Xbiex

Christopher's (expensive *à la carte*) *Ta'Xbiex marina, next door to the Yacht Centre* ☎ 337 101 High-class restaurant, dishes exquisitely cooked, with a good selection of starters and meat dishes (try the fettucini with wild mushrooms and roast sea scallops as a starter). Elegant and comfortable setting (open Tuesday to Saturday).

Gozo
Xagħra
The Oleander (inexpensive) *Victory Square* ☎ 557 230 Authentic Gozitan food, in a pleasant local establishment; good value.

Għarb
Salvina (moderate) *21 Triq il-Blata* ☎ 552 505 Very attractive restaurant in rustic house serving Gozitan food (open for dinner only; closed on Thursdays).

Recommendations for snacks or for a drink
Ciappetti Tea Gardens (Mdina) A very pleasant place to stop when exploring Mdina's medieval streets, for a glass of kinnie or a tasty snack (try *hobz biz-zejt*). Vaulted rooms and patio with flowers, and a terrace on the ramparts.

Fontanella (Mdina) Café set in a garden, right on the ramparts of Mdina, with views of Mosta and its famous dome in one direction, and to Valletta in the other.

Caffe Teatro and Ristorante de Vilhena *Old Theatre St, Valletta* ☎ 223 005 Situated next door to the Manoel Theatre, with a lovely patio.

Caffe Cordina *Republic Street, Valletta* Renowned café with Baroque interior and terrace on Republic Square. Try the *pastizzi* with ricotta, or choose from the large selection of sorbets and cakes.

French-style Wine & Cheese Bar/Spanish Tapas Bar *Corinthia Beach Resort, St George's Bay* Try a glass of Malqart 1996 – made of Merlot and Cabernet Sauvignon – with goats' cheese on toast at the wine bar, or tuck into a variety of tapas.

SHOPPING

Malta is not a shopper's island – indeed, many Maltese take a day trip to Sicily when they feel the urge to shop. Usually Maltese crafts are the best buys; the islanders have a long tradition of arts and crafts, inherited from the Knights who developed the local skills in weaving, pottery, gold and silver working, glass-blowing and lace-making partly to meet their own increasingly luxurious lifestyles and partly for trade with Europe.

There are two **craft villages**: Ta'Qali near the airport on Malta, and Ta'Dbiegi just outside Gharb on Gozo. The range of Maltese goods on offer is reasonable, though their settings – for some reason both are housed in breeze-block huts in prison-camp-like compounds – are somewhat depressing. At **Ta'Qali** you can visit around 20 workshops and see the craftsmen at work before making your choice from the goods on offer. Coach parties stop off here on tours of the island but it's more pleasant to visit independently and browse at your leisure. The **Ta'Dbiegi** centre on Gozo is similar, but smaller, with the emphasis on lace-making and weaving. In Valletta, the **Malta Government Craft Centre**, opposite St John's Co-Cathedral, opens during the summer months for the display and sale of crafts. At the **Empire Art and Crafts Centre** (*20A St Agatha Street, Rabat*) you can also watch craftsmen making glass and filigree goods, together with lace-making and weaving, following your visit with wine-tasting at the Empire Cafeteria.

Away from the austere settings of the craft villages, it's far cheerier to stroll through Valletta where you will find small specialist shops with beautiful façades that look as if they have been untouched since the war. Indeed, most Maltese shops are small, family-run businesses where change is slow to happen. This is the place to buy silver filigree jewellery, Maltese stamps, glassware and other island specialities from enthusiastic shop-owners who know their business.

If you are British, don't waste your time at Marks & Spencer and other UK-transplanted shops – you will find the same goods cheaper at home.

Note that most shops close for a siesta from 1pm-4pm, when they re-open until 7pm. They are closed from 1pm Saturday until Monday morning. In the tourist centres, however, they may open all day, every day.

Markets

The markets in Valletta provide the best local colour, though even this is limited. The much-vaunted Sunday morning flea market, just outside the City Gate, is full of cheap household goods and counterfeit Far-Eastern products, and does not provide particularly good shopping. That said, there's a lively bustle to it and it is still worth a visit to see a slice of everyday Maltese life. The daily market on Triq Merkanti (Merchants' Street) features much the same style of merchandise. Pop into the indoor market on the same street to catch the colourful fruit and vegetables stands and delicatessens.

Rabat has a daily market, and Marsaxlokk market, set in front of the church, might be worth a visit if you are looking for lace, though it has little else. On Gozo you may pick up cheap woollens at Victoria's small daily market in It-Tokk Square.

What to Buy

Lace is the island speciality; look out for tablecloths, napkins, shawls and handkerchiefs. Lace-makers are a dying breed on the islands and you should beware of imitations from the Far East. Let price, and a close inspection of quality, be your guide.

Glassware is the island's most striking product, often in beautiful hues of gold and brown or blue. Pay a visit to the Phoenicia Glassblowers on Manoel Island, opposite the Sliema ferries (complimentary boats shuttle to and fro), and also to Gozo

A Maltese grocer carts his fresh fare around Rabat.

Glass at Għarb, on Gozo. Maltese blown glass is not cheap but the quality is good and you can see the pieces made right in front of your eyes.

More portable and often just as beautiful is the filigree **silver and gold** jewellery produced by Maltese artisans. You can see them at work in many places; Valletta has the best choice of such shops. This is often very good value.

If the weather turns cold or the wind blows hard you'll appreciate the islands' **woollens**, particularly the chunky knitted jumpers found on Gozo and the main island, often at very reasonable prices.

Other items to look for are brass and iron door knockers, often in a dolphin shape, reproducing the old styles found in historical places like Mdina. There is a long tradition of **metalworking** on Malta going back to the Knights of St John. You can even have your very own suit of armour made!

More easily transported home is the delicious local **honey**, characteristically flavoured by the wild thyme that the bees feed on. Similarly, the island's **capers** will help you to take home the memories of Maltese cuisine with you.

ENTERTAINMENT AND NIGHTLIFE

Excursions

The main operator for a variety of excursions and tours is Captain Morgan Cruises, Dolphin Court, Tigné Seafront, Sliema, Malta ☎ 343 373/331 961/336 981. In addition to the boat trips and cruises, the company also offers jeep safaris and helicopter rides.

By Boat

With glorious blue seas but relatively few beaches, boat trips are a perennially popular way of spending a full or half day around the islands. Of those offered by Captain Morgan, there are several options: *Around the Islands*; *Comino's Blue Lagoon* (*see* p.90); *Underwater Safaris* (*see* p.70); and, for the young and carefree, *Booze Cruises and Party Nights*, with all drinks included in the price. There are various types of craft to choose from: a Turkish *gulet*, a sail-catamaran and a square-sail two-masted schooner, or you can charter your own yacht.

Two shorter boat trips that should not be missed are the Grand Harbour tour (*see* p.24) and The Blue Grotto (*see* p.55). Don't forget your sunblock – it can be breezy on deck and you may not realise how strong the sun is.

Other Tours

Jeep safaris are a fun, if highly uncomfortable, way to see those parts of the island where 2-wheel drive cars fear to tread, and budding rally drivers may get to take the wheel themselves.

A much more sedate trip is a tour of the Three Cities aboard a smart 1920s bus (*see* p.39). Book both through Captain Morgan or your travel representative.

Helicopter Flights

Though much of Malta looks untidy and uneven from ground level, the view from above is very different. Unforgettable is Valletta, where you can see the die-straight street grid patterns and the scrum of buses outside City Gate. It is possibly only from above that you can really appreciate the enormity of Valletta's awe-inspiring fortifications and marvellous natural harbours. The dramatic sheer cliffs of the island and the often huge churches which dwarf the tiny villages they serve are other highlights.

Fabulous!

Flights last either 20 or 40 minutes. The latter is recommended as time literally flies once you are in the air. Departures are from Luqa airport, with a 30-minute check in. Book through Captain Morgan or your travel representative.

To Sicily

The beautiful island of Sicily lies just 90 minutes away by express catamaran ferry, and full-day excursion tours include a visit to Mount Etna and the splendidly situated town of Taormina, with its panoramic views from its famous hilltop *teatro greco* amphitheatre. Book at any Oasis Tours travel agent.

Family Attractions

There may not be a lot of sandy beaches, and there are surprisingly few children's entertainments in Malta, but the Maltese people love children and will make them very welcome. Add to that the abundant sunshine and the clean blue sea for swimming, and the island certainly has an appeal for families.

The various audio-visual spectaculars depicting the island's history will undoubtedly appeal to youngsters, who will be absorbed by the special effects, if not the historical facts. Try **The Malta Experience**, the

Knights Hospitallers, the **Valletta Experience** and **Malta George Cross**, all in Valletta (*see* pp.29, 30, 34); or **The Knights of Malta**, **Medieval Times**, **The Mdina Experience** and **Mdina Dungeons** (not for the very young) in Mdina (*see* p.60).

Popeye Village is a highlight, though even this is arguably an adult attraction (*see* p.74).

Another popular day out is the **Splash and Fun Water Park** (open summer only), about 10km (6 miles) north of Valletta

Colourful 'In Guardia' historical re-enactment, Fort St Elmo, Valletta.

on the coast road to St Paul's Bay at Bahar-ic-caghaq (White Rocks). Adjacent is **Mediterraneo Marine World**, a marine park featuring dolphin and sea lion shows, sea birds and an open air aquarium (open daily, all year). Teenagers will enjoy 10-pin bowling at **Eden Super Bowl**, at St George's Bay.

In Guardia! (*see* p.31) is an enjoyable pageant for all the family which is staged at Fort St Elmo regularly throughout the year. For dates of the parades, contact the National Tourism Organisation.

A recent attraction is the

Rinella Movie Park, near the village of Kalkara, north of Vittoriosa, where you can explore one of the largest film studios in the Mediterranean and see where parts of films, including *Orca*, *Midnight Express* and *Raise the Titanic*, were filmed. The 'Screening Theatre' explains in detail how many of the spectacular scenes from famous films were shot. The open-air tram tour takes in the 9 million gallon marine filming tank, and there are play areas and a Pirate Alley market for the children to explore.

Keep an eye open for fly posters which advertise local events such as *festas* and visiting Italian circuses.

Nightlife

The island's only traditional nightlife is apparent at *festa* time, when whole villages break into processions and street parties. Festivities are topped off with a spectacular flourish of fireworks. Visitors are welcome and enterprising tour operators ensure a bus is always on hand to transport holidaymakers to and from most *festas*. During the summer these happen almost on a weekly basis, so you have a good chance of catching one. Out of summer the liveliest event of the year is Carnival (*see* p.92).

The nightlife capital of the island is **Paceville**, by St Julian's Bay. Here there is an enormous number of music bars, most pumping out high-decibel Euro-thump. As the night wears on, the focus of attention switches to the two giant nightclubs, Axis and Euphoria, which attract the cream of Europe's DJs on a regular basis. Every night, youthful holidaymakers and the Maltese themselves pack in here to party until dawn.

Close by at the Dragonara Hotel, by St George's Bay, Malta's only **casino** attracts an older and wealthier class of visitor. If you fancy a flutter, either at the gaming tables or on the slot machines, you will need to wear a collar and tie, take your passport and be 18 years or older.

For a cultural evening, check what is on at Valletta's **Manoel Theatre** (☎ 222 618). This little gem (*see* p.35) stages regular productions of ballet, opera concerts and plays (though rarely in English). A free lunchtime concert is held in one of the theatre's recital rooms every Wednesday.

Other evening options include one of the island's many cinemas and 10-pin bowling at the Eden Super Bowl in St George's Bay (☎ 319 888).

SPORT

Taking part

The island's clear blue waters, healthy underwater fauna and flora, and warm summer seas (averaging 23°C/74°F) mean **diving** is very popular. The scarcity of sand, lack of pollution and stillness of the virtually tide-free waters all contribute to excellent visibility, which on average is up to 30m (100ft). There are caves and grottoes to explore and good wreck-diving. Diving clubs on the island operate to a high standard, and are well equipped to deal with beginners and qualified divers. You can also hire equipment at reasonable rates.

There are numerous diving centres on both Malta and Gozo, and a list of these can be obtained from the Malta Tourist Office at home or from the National Tourism Organisation in Valletta (☎ 222 444/5). They include: Dive Systems, Sliema (☎ 319 123); Cresta Diving Centre, St George's Bay (☎ 310 743); Divewise Services, Dragonara Water Sports Centre, St Julian's (☎ 336 441); and Calypso Aquatic Sports Club, Marina Street, Marsalforn, Gozo (☎ 562 000).

At Golden Bay and Mellieħa Bay you will find the usual range of popular **watersports** facilities: windsurfers, water-skiing and jet skis. Experienced windsurfers should head for Mellieħa. Non-skilled thrill-seekers can also paraglide and ride inflatables.

There is only one **golf** course on Malta, the 18-hole Royal Malta Club at Marsa Sports Club. Equipment is available for hire. This complex also includes 19 **tennis** courts, five

Delving the depths can reveal all sorts of marine life! Diving in Xlendi, Gozo.

squash courts, mini-golf, an open-air **swimming** pool and billiards. Weekly membership is available at the Marsa Sports Club, situated on the outskirts of Marsa, open to visitors from 8am-3pm, with the golf course open from 8am-sunset (except on competition days). Booking is essential for use of all facilities (☎ 233 851).

Many hotels are equipped with tennis courts for the use of their guests. The Hotel Comino is a good place for tennis with ten courts, though it is hardly accessible for a casual game!

Horse-riding, both for experienced riders and beginners, is available at Golden Bay and follows enjoyable beach-side trails. There are also several riding schools in the area around the Marsa racecourse and some hotels offer horse-riding facilities.

Spectating

Horse-racing, of the trotting variety, is the most popular spectator sport in Malta. Jockeys do not ride the horses but are pulled along on a flimsy-looking trap. The course is at Marsa and the 12-race meetings on summer Sundays pulls in crowds of up to 4 000 (racing continues throughout the year). You can bet on the tote or direct with the 'bookies'.

Waterpolo is another Maltese speciality and you can see top-quality league games staged in the 'pitches' on the seafront of many resorts in summer.

Football is another popular sport among locals, with the National Football Stadium located in Ta'Qali. Not to be outdone, Gozo has a splendid ground in Victoria, with a special astroturf-type surface.

Jockeys pull in the crowds at the trotting races, Marsa.

THE BASICS

Before You Go
Visitors entering Malta should have a full passport valid to cover the period in which they will be travelling. No visa is required for members of EU countries. Citizens of the Republic of Ireland, the US, Canada, Australia and New Zealand can stay for up to three months without a visa. No vaccinations are necessary.

Getting There
By Air
Malta has only one airport, at Luqa in the centre of the island, 6km (3.7 miles) south of Valletta. This handles international flights and domestic flights to Gozo. There are several direct charter and scheduled flights to Malta from all over Europe, particularly the UK. The national carrier is **Air Malta**.
For enquiries in the UK ☎ **(020) 7292 4949**; reservations can be made on **(020) 8785 3177**. The Air Malta offices in Malta are located in Freedom Square, Valletta ☎ **240 686/7/8**, and at Luqa airport ☎ **690 890**. For reservations in Malta ☎ **662 211/6**. There are no direct flights from the United States or Canada, and visitors from these countries will have to make connections in Europe.

By Ferry
The **Gozo Channel Company** operates a weekly foot-passenger and car-ferry service between Malta and Catania (Sicily) in April and June, with increased frequency throughout the rest of the summer months. Cruising time is around 8 hours.

Virtu Ferries operates high-speed catamaran passenger-only services to Sicily (Syracuse, Catania, Licata and Pozzallo). They operate between March and October, but less frequently at either side of the high season. The approximate length of journey is around 3 hours. For details contact Virtu Rapid Ferries, 3 Princess Elizabeth Street, Ta'Xbiex ☎ **345 220**.

The **Ma.Re.Si Shipping Co Ltd** operates a car ferry service between Malta and Catania, Sicily, (twice weekly, departing from Valletta on Mondays and Wednesdays), and to Reggio di Calabria on mainland Italy (once weekly, departing from Valletta on Fridays, and from Reggio di Calabria on Sundays). For further details contact Ma. Re. Si Shipping c/o SMS Travel & Tourism, 131 East Street, Valletta ☎ **233 129**.

Arriving

Non-Maltese travellers must complete an embarkation card before passing passport control. From Luqa airport there is a regular and frequent bus service to many parts of the island. The journey to Valletta, by bus nos 8, takes about 20 minutes. Taxis are also available (*see* **Transport**).

Karrozins take a breather, Valletta.

A-Z

Accidents and Breakdowns

Contact the rental firm in the event of an accident or breakdown. If you have an accident, exchange names, addresses and insurance details but on no account move the vehicle, even if you are causing a hold up, as this may affect your insurance claim. To contact the police on Malta ☎ 191; (in Gozo ☎ 562 040) ambulance ☎ 196

See also **Driving**, **Emergencies**

Accommodation see p.95

Airports see Getting There, p.112

Banks

Banks are open approximately 8/8.30am–1/2pm, Mon-Fri (some open until 3pm in winter), and until around noon on Saturday. They are closed on Sundays and national holidays. A passport is required if you are changing money. Many major banks have a money-changing desk open

in the afternoons. Luqa airport bureau de change is open 24 hours. Automated teller machines (ATMs) can be found in the resorts and in Valletta. Travellers' cheques and cash can also be changed at most hotels, although the exchange rate may not be very favourable.

Bicycles

Cycle-hire outlets can be found in the resorts. Beware that the standard of driving and the poor condition of the roads can make this a very hazardous way of getting around.

Books

Here are a few suggested titles for your holiday reading:
The Great Siege – Malta 1565, Ernle Bradford, Penguin Books
Siege of Malta 1940-43, Ernle Bradford, Penguin Books
The Kappillan of Malta, Nicholas Monsarrat, Pan (London)
Foucault's Pendulum, Umberto Eco, Secker & Warburg

Breakdowns see **Accidents**

Camping
There are no organised or official camping sites on the islands.

Car Hire
The airport and resorts have numerous international and local car-hire agencies. Rates are among the cheapest in Europe. Accidents are frequent so you are strongly advised to take out collision damage waiver.

Air Malta's Flydrive deals include collision damage waiver, unlimited mileage and taxes, and can be booked at the same time as your flight ticket, or through Budget Rent-a-Car Malta, Marsa ☎ 241 517/231 077/242 799/221 888. The small, local firms generally offer the cheapest rates, but they can be booked only locally.

Most companies restrict hire of cars to drivers over 25 and under 70. Drivers must have held a full licence for at least a year. Unless paying by credit card, a substantial cash deposit is required. *See also* **Driving**, **Accidents and Breakdowns**

Churches see **Religion**

Climate see **p.92**

Clothing
Spring and autumn are warm and pleasant times of the year to visit Malta, and during those months light clothes can be worn in the day, with an extra sweater or jacket for the evenings and cooler days. The summer months are very hot indeed. Winters are mild by European standards, with a good deal of sunshine, but you will still need some warm clothing.

Casual wear is generally acceptable, although smarter clothing will not be out of place at 5-star hotels and more exclusive restaurants. Remember when visiting churches that bare legs and

Ornate door-knocker, Mdina.

arms will still be frowned upon
(they may even be forbidden).

Most clothing measurements
are standard throughout
Europe but differ from those
in the UK and the US. The
following are examples:

Women's sizes

UK	8	10	12	14	16	18
Europe	38	40	42	44	46	48
US	6	8	10	12	14	16

Women's shoes

UK	4.5	5	5.5	6	6.5	7
Europe	38	38	39	39	40	41
US	6	6.5	7	7.5	8	8.5

Men's suits

UK/US	36	38	40	42	44	46
Europe	46	48	50	52	54	56

Men's shirts

UK/US	14	14.5	15	15.5	16	16.5	17
Europe	36	37	38	39/40	41	42	43

Men's shoes

UK	7	7.5	8.5	9.5	10.5	11
Europe	41	42	43	44	45	46
US	8	8.5	9.5	10.5	11.5	12

Consulates, Embassies and High Commissions
Australia
Australian High Commission
Ta'Xbiex Terrace, Ta'Xbiex
☎ 338 201/5
UK
British High Commission
7 St Anne Street, Floriana
☎ 233 134/8
Canada
Canadian Consulate
103 Archbishop Street, Valletta
☎ 233 122

Embassies
France
Villa Seminia, 12 Sir Temi
Zammit Street, Ta'Xbiex
☎ 331 107
Spain
145/10 Tower Road, Sliema
☎ 314 164/5
US
Development House, 3rd
Floor, St Anne Street, Floriana
☎ 235 961/5

Crime
One of the attractions of Malta
is its lack of crime. Nonetheless,
it is advisable to take sensible
precautions and be on your
guard at all times. The main
hazard is theft from cars, particularly where they are left
unattended at beaches. At
some places the locals clear
their cars of all contents and
leave the windows open so that
these are not smashed to force
entry. At other places, however,
unofficial attendants will be on
hand to help park your car and
look after it. It's common
courtesy to give them a small
tip (10-25 cents).

If you are concerned about
security remember the following guidelines:
• Carry as little money and as
few credit cards as possible,
and leave any valuables in the
hotel safe.
• Carry wallets and purses in

secure pockets inside your outer clothing, and carry handbags across your body or firmly under your arm.

• Cars should never be left unlocked, and you should remove items of value.

• If your passport is lost or stolen, report it to your holiday representative, Consulate or Embassy at once.

Currency see Money

Customs and Entry Regulations

Personal belongings and clothing intended for your own use are not liable to duty. The duty-free allowance for adults is 200 cigarettes or the equivalent in cigars or tobacco; one bottle of spirits and one bottle of wine, and a reasonable amount of perfume and toilet water.

Disabled Visitors

In Britain, RADAR, at 12 City Forum, 250 City Road, London EC1V 8AF ☎ (020) 7250 3222, publishes factsheets as well as an annual guide to facilities and accommodation overseas, including Malta.

Valletta, Mdina and Victoria (Gozo) with their cobbled streets and numerous steps, are difficult for those in wheelchairs, and few museums have disabled access. The Malta Tourist Offices can also give information about visitor facilities (see **Tourist Information Offices**). In Malta, the Physically Handicapped Rehabilitation Fund offers advice to visitors ☎ **693 863**.

Driving

The standard of driving in Malta is notoriously bad. Remember to drive on the LEFT, and to give way to traffic coming from the right – although you will soon notice that some drivers take no notice of this rule (or indeed, any rules).

Street parking is always difficult and, if there is one, it is

No loafing about in this traditional wood-fired bakery, Qormi.

best to use an official car park. Never leave valuables in the car as theft is common.

Petrol stations are frequent and are generally open daily from 7am-6/6.30pm. A few also open later (and during public holidays) on a rota basis. Check the local newspaper for details. On Sundays most petrol stations operate on a self-service basis until 10pm. Unleaded petrol is commonly available. Small petrol stations may not accept credit cards.

There are no motorways and road surfaces are often poor; in rural areas and on Gozo they may be heavily pot-holed. Signposting is just about adequate for the main routes, but off the beaten track may be non-existent. The following speed limits apply:
Highways 64kph/40mph
Built-up areas 40kph/25mph

Drivers should carry a full national or international driving licence. In the event that you are taking your own car, also take insurance documents including a green card (no longer compulsory for EU members but strongly recommended), registration papers for the car and a nationality sticker for the rear of the car.

Headlight beams should be adjusted for left-hand drive, and a red warning triangle must be carried unless there are hazard warning lights on the car. You should also have a spare set of light bulbs.

The wearing of seatbelts is compulsory (although few Maltese bother); children between nine months and four years must be seated in the back, babies up to nine months must occupy a baby seat. *See also* **Accidents and Breakdowns**

Electric Current
The voltage in Malta is usually 240V. Plugs and sockets are of the square-fitting three-pin British variety.

Embassies see Consulates

Emergencies
Malta
Police ☎ 191
Ambulance ☎ 196
Fire ☎ 199
General Hospital ☎ 561 600
Gozo
Police and fire ☎ 562 040
Ambulance ☎ 556 851

Etiquette
When visiting churches, visitors should remember that they are places of worship and should dress discreetly, covering upper legs and arms. The Maltese are usually a friendly and courteous people, although they are slightly more restrained than

other southern Europeans.

Women travelling alone should have few problems and will receive much less unwanted attention than in other places, though they should take the usual precautions.

Guidebooks see **Maps**

Health

The high-quality services of state-run hospitals and clinics are available free of charge to visitors who come from a country which has a reciprocal health care agreement. This includes the UK and Australia. All you need is your passport. All foreign nationals are advised to take out comprehensive insurance cover and to keep any bills, receipts and invoices to support any claim.

Lists of doctors can be obtained from hotels, chemists or by looking in the newspaper. Beware of the intense heat in July and August.

Enjoying the sun at Café Fontanella on the ramparts of Mdina.

Hours see **Opening Hours**

Information see **Tourist Information Offices**

Language

The official languages are Maltese (Malti) and English. The vast majority of Maltese speak English, and Italian is also widely spoken. Malti comprises elements of Arabic, English, Italian and French. It is difficult for the visitor to master but any effort to speak even a few simple words and expressions is often warmly received. Below are a few words and phrases to help you make the most of your stay:

Place name pronunciations

Buġibba	boo-jee-bah
Dwejra	d'way-rah
Ġgantija	jee-gan-tee-yah
Għar...	ahr...
Għarb	ahrb
Ħaġar Qim	ha-jah eem
Luqa	loo-ah
Marsaxlokk	marsa-shlock
Mdina	im-deenah
Mellieħa	mell-ee-ah
Mġarr	im-jar
Msida	im-see-dah
Naxxar	nash-shar
Paceville	parch-ay-ville
Qawra	ou-rah
Ta'Ċenċ	ta-chench
Tarxien	tar-she-en
Xagħra	shar-rur
Xewkija	show-key-yah
Xlendi	shlen-dee

English	Malti	pronounced
Yes	Iva	ee-va
No	Le	le (e, as in egg)
Please	Jekk-joghgbok	yeck yojbok
Thank you	Grazzi	gra-tsee
Good morning	Bonju	bon-jew
Good evening	Bonswa	bon-swa
Goodbye	Sahha	sa-ha
How much?	Kemm?	kem?
Where is …?	Fejn hu …?	fen-oo?
Do you speak English?	Titkellem bl-Ingliz?	tit kel-lem bling-lis?
I don't understand	ma nifimx	ma nif-imsh

Maps
The tourist offices provide free plans of Valletta, Buġibba, Sliema and St Julian's, and a basic map of the island.

Michelin on the net:
www.michelin-travel.com
Our route-planning service covers all of Europe. Options allow you to choose a pre-ferred route and these are updated three times weekly, integrating on-going road-works etc. The descriptions include distances and travel-ling times between towns, selected hotels and restaurants.

Money
The monetary unit of Malta is the Maltese lira (Lm). There are 100 cents to the lire. Notes are issued in denominations of Lm2, Lm5, Lm10 and Lm20. Coins are Lm1 and 1, 2, 5, 10, 25 and 50 cents. All major credit cards – American Express, Carte Bleue (Visa/Barclaycard), Diners Club and Eurocard (Mastercard/Access) – travellers' cheques and Eurocheques are accepted in most shops, restaurants and hotels, but not always at petrol stations.

There are no restrictions on the amount of foreign currency visitors can take into Malta, providing it is declared on arrival; however, only a maximum of Lm50 may be imported. The safest way to carry large amounts of money is in travellers' cheques which are widely accepted. Bureaux de change desks are found at the airport and banks (*see also* **Banks**).

Exchange rates vary so it pays to shop around. Try not to pay hotel bills in foreign currency or with travellers' cheques since the hotel's exchange rate is likely to be higher than that of the bureaux de change.

Newspapers
British and foreign newspapers and magazines can be bought in the main towns at newsagents and kiosks, usually the same day.

The local daily papers are useful for tourists as they include leisure sections, trans-port timetables, and other relevant practical information.

Opening Hours
Shops: Traditional shop opening hours are 9am-1pm and 4-7pm Mon-Sat. In tourist areas, however, many open until 10pm and may remain open throughout the day. They may well also open on Sunday.
Chemists: These are generally open 8.30/9am-1pm and

3/4-7pm, Mon-Sat. Lists of chemists which are open late or on Sundays can be found in the newspapers.

Museums: The opening hours for National Museums, which also includes several important archaeological sites, are as follows:

Malta
1 Oct-15 June:
Mon-Sat 8.15am-5pm
Sun 8.15am-4pm
16 June-30 Sept:
Mon-Sat 7.45am-2pm
Closed Sunday

Gozo
1 Oct-31 Mar:
Mon-Sat 8.30am-4.30pm
1 April-15 June:
Mon-Sat 8.30am-6.30pm
16 June-15 Sept:
Mon-Sat 8.30am-7pm
16 Sept-30 Sept:
Mon-Sat 8.30am-6.30pm
All year: Sundays 8.30am-3pm

Other (privately owned) attractions are usually open daily from around 9am to 5pm or 6pm, sometimes closing for an hour or two for lunch.

Churches: Hours vary but many are closed in the middle

A window on the world – charming terraced balconies.

of the day or open only for services. *See also* **Banks**, **Post Offices**

Photography
Good-quality film and camera equipment are readily available, at comparable prices with the UK (though developing costs more). Before taking photographs in museums you should check with staff, as photography is often restricted. Never leave cameras in cars.

Police
Police officers wear a black uniform in winter and khaki in summer. They are usually friendly and approachable. Police stations can be found in all villages and towns.
For police assistance ☎ 191 (in Gozo ☎ 562 040).

Post Offices
Post offices are usually open 7.45am-1.30pm, Mon-Fri, 9am-noon on Saturday, but times vary. The main post office, in Valletta on Merchants' Street, opens until 6pm Mon-Sat.
    Stamps are sold in post offices, by newsagents, hotels and tobacconists (*tabacchi*) which display a black sign with a white 'T'.

Public Holidays
New Year's Day: 1 January

St Paul's Shipwreck: 10 February
Feast of St Joseph: 19 March
Freedom Day: 31 March
Good Friday: variable
Workers' Day: 1 May
Commemoration of 7 June 1919: 7 June
Feast of St Peter and St Paul: 29 June
Assumption Day: 15 August
Feast of Our Lady of Victories: 8 September
Independence Day: 21 September
Immaculate Conception: 8 December
Republic Day: 13 December
Christmas Day: 25 December

Religion
Malta is a Roman Catholic country and mass is celebrated in most churches every Sunday. For details of services in other languages, or of churches of other denominations, contact the local tourist information office or ask at your hotel.

Smoking
Smoking is banned in most public places though this rule is flouted almost everywhere. Tobacconists (*tabacchi*) sell the major international brands of cigarettes, which are also on sale in bars.

Telephones

Kiosks take telephone cards to the value of Lm2-5, sold at newsagents and tobacconists, or 10, 25 or 50 cents coins. You can dial anywhere in Malta and abroad from street telephone boxes. Calls and faxes can also be made from the offices of the Maltacom company who have various branches including: St George's Road (open 24-hour) and Park Tower, St Julian's; Triq Nofs-in-Nhar, Valletta; Luqa airport; Bisazza Street and Sliema Plaza on Tower Road, Sliema; Triq San Pawl, St Paul's Bay; Triq Fliegu, Qawra; and Republic Street, Victoria on Gozo. The call is metered and you pay afterwards.

As in most countries, telephone calls made from hotels may be more straightforward and convenient but they are much more expensive.

Cheap rates apply 9pm-8am, Mon-Sat, and all day Sunday. For local directory enquiries ☎ 190

For international operator and international directory enquiries ☎ 194.

Country codes are as follows:
Australia: ☎ 00 61
Canada: ☎ 00 1
Ireland: ☎ 00 353
New Zealand: ☎ 00 64
UK: ☎ 00 44

USA: ☎ 00 1

To call Malta from abroad, ☎ 00 356

Time Difference

Malta is on Central European Time, one hour ahead of Greenwich Mean Time (GMT) in winter and 2 hours ahead from the last Sunday in March to the last Sunday in September. It is always one hour ahead of the time in the UK. The islands are six hours ahead of US Eastern Standard Winter Time and seven hours ahead in summer.

Tipping

If a service charge (usually 10 or 15 per cent) is not included in the restaurant bill, and the service has been good, then leave a tip of around 10 per cent. It is also customary to tip hotel-room maids Lm1-2 per week. Taxi drivers will expect about 10 per cent.

Tourist Information Offices

The Malta National Tourist Office is a good initial source of information before you go, including accommodation, travel and places of interest:
UK: Malta Tourist Office, Malta House, 36-38 Piccadilly, London W1V 0PP
☎ (020) 7292 4900
US and Canada: Malta

National Tourist Office, Empire State Building, 350 Fifth Avenue, Suite 4412, New York, NY 10118 ☎ (212) 695 9520 In Malta, the headquarters of the National Tourism Organisation is at 280 Republic Street, Valletta ☎ 224 444/5.

There are tourist information offices at:

Malta International Airport ☎ 249 600/4

1 City Gate, Valletta ☎ 237 747

1 Palm Street, Victoria, Gozo ☎ 558 106

Mġarr Harbour, Gozo ☎ 553 343

Or check out the internet site at: www.visitmalta.com

Tours

Practically all travel agents in the major resorts offer a number of organised tours. Most of the major hotels also offer coach and boat tours covering the islands' highlights (*see* p.106).

Transport

Hiring a car obviously gives you the greatest flexibility, but driving on Maltese roads is not for the faint-hearted (*see* **Driving**).

Bus: The cheapest and easiest way of getting around Malta is aboard its fleet of antiquated buses. They provide a reliable, if slow and sometimes uncomfortably crowded, service. Most

Checking out directions.

services terminate in Valletta, where you have to change to continue your journey. However, there are a number of 'point-to-point' services, some of which are designed specifically for visitors and run in summer only. You can pick up a list of routes from the small kiosk at the Valletta terminal or from a tourist office. Tickets are bought aboard the bus (have small change to hand) and generally cost a maximum of 16 cents. There are no multi-journey tickets or passes for visitors at present but these may be introduced in 1999. In Gozo, buses radiate out from Victoria but services are infrequent.

Boat: The Gozo Channel Company (Malta ☎ 243 964/5/6; Gozo ☎ 556 114) operates a frequent daily foot-passenger and car-ferry service between Cirkewwa (Malta ☎ 580 435/6) and Mġarr (Gozo ☎ 556 114). The crossing takes around 30 minutes. From July-September the same company runs a passenger-only hover-marine service between Sa Maison dock at Sliema and Gozo. This takes approximately 25 minutes.

Taxis: These can generally be found in special taxi ranks or your hotel will call one for you. Most are in white livery (though some are black) with distinctive red number plates. Taxis cannot usually be hailed in the street. Fares from the airport are regulated and prominently displayed; elsewhere it's a case of 'buyer beware'. Make sure the taxi meter is either switched on or that you have agreed a fare in advance. Fares increase steeply after midnight, which is, not coincidentally, generally the only time you will need a taxi.

TV and Radio

Malta has its own national channel broadcasting in Malti. There are also several Italian channels available. Cable and satellite television is common in hotels and bars. For news, documentaries and chat in English, listen to Radio Malta 1 (999MW), Radio Malta 2 (93.7FM) or tune into one of the commercial pop and chat shows on the FM band. See the local press for details of programmes.

Vaccinations
see **Before You Go p.112**

Water

Generally, tap water is safe to drink although it often doesn't taste very pleasant and bottled water is the popular alternative.

INDEX

accommodation 95
Anchor Bay 74
Armier Bay (Il-Bajja ta'l-
    Armier) 73
Attard 66-67
    Church of St Mary 67
auberges 26, 27

Birżebbuġa 54, 55
Blue Grotto 21, 55-56
boat trips 45, 106
British rule 11, 18-19
Buġibba 69
Buskett Gardens 6, 56, 57

Captain Morgan 70, 106
Caravaggio 38
Carthaginians 8
Cirkewwa 73-74
Clapham Junction 77
Comino 6, 8, 90-91
    Blue Lagoon 90
    Knights' lookout tower 91
    San Niklaw Bay 91
Cominotto 6
Cospicua (Bormla) 39
Cottonera Lines 40, 48

Dingli 6, 57
Dingli Cliffs 57
diving 110

Eden Super Bowl 108, 109

festa 92, 109
festivals 92-94
filfla 6
food and drink 98
Fort Ricasoli 31

Gnejna Bay (Il-Bajja tal-
    Gnejna) 75
George Cross 15, 31
Ghadira Beach 72
Ghadira Nature Reserve 73
Ghajn Tuffieha Bay (Ir-Ramla
    ta'Ghajn Tuffieha) 75
Ghar Dalam (Cave of
    Darkness) 53, 54
Ghar Lapsi 57
Golden Bay (Ir-Ramla tal-
    Mixquqa) 75
Gozo 6, 8, 22, 78-90
    Azure Window 85
    Calypso's Cave 88
    Dahlet Qorrot 89

Dwejra Point (Il Ponta tad-
    Dwejra) 6, 85
Fort Chambray 79-80
Fungus Rock (Gebla
    tal'General) 85
Ġgantija 22, 76-77, 89
Gharb 18, 84
    Church of the Immaculate
        Conception 84
    Folklore Museum 84
    Gozo Glass 84
Gozo Heritage 80
Inland Sea (Il Qawra) 85, 86
Knights' Wash House 86
Mgarr 79
    Our Lady of Lourdes 79
Marsalforn 87
Mgarr-ix-Xini 87
Pomskizillious Toy Museum
    89-90
Qawra Tower 86
Ramla Bay (Ir-Ramla) 88
San Blas 88
Ta' Pinu Basilica 83, 84
Ta'Cenc 87
Ta'Kola Windmill Museum
    89
Victoria (Rabat) 22, 81-83
    Archaeological Museum 82
    Cathedral 22, 82
    Citadel (Il-Kastell) 22, 81
    Folklore Museum 82
    Gozo 360°
    Knights' Armoury 82
    Natural History Museum
        82
    Pjazza d'Independenza
        (Independence Square
        81)
    Rundle Gardens 81
    St George's Basilica 82-83
Xerri's Grotto 89
Xewkija 80
    Rotunda Church 80
Xaghra 89
Xlendi 86-86
Great Siege 10, 12-13, 23, 31,
    81

Hal Saflieni Hypogeum 20,
    50
Hagar Qim 56
Homepesch Arch 49

Inquisitor's Summer Palace
    58

Knights of St John 10-11, 12-
    13, 23, 25, 30, 31, 34, 35,
    37, 40, 58, 60

Lija 66, 67

Mgarr 75, 76
Manoel Island 45
    Phoenician Glassblowers
        Factory 45
Marfa Ridge 72-73
markets 105
Marsamxett 97
Marsaskala (Wied-Il-Ghajn)
    51, 52-53
Marsaxlokk 22, 51, 53
Marsaxlokk Bay (Il Bajja ta'-
    Marsaxlokk) 52, 53
Mattia Preti 36, 38, 41
Mdina 22, 58-63, 115, 119
    Bastion Square 63
    Cathedral of St Peter and St
        Paul 22, 61, 62
    city gates 60
    museums
        Cathedral Museum 62
        Knights of Malta 60, 108
        Mdina Experienc 60, 108
        Mdina Dungeons 61, 108
        Medieval Times 60, 108
        Museum of Natural History
            61
    Palazzo Falzon 62
    Triq Villegaignon 59, 60, 61,
        62, 63
    Vilhena Palace 61
Mediterraneo Marine World
    108
Mellieha 72
    Nativity of Our Lady 72
Mellieha Bay (Il Bajja tal-
    Mellieha) 72
Mnajdra 56
Mosta 68
    Mosta Dome 22, 68
Msida Creek 45

Naxxar 68-69
    International Fair 69
    Palazzo Parisio 69

Paceville 47, 109
Peter's Pool 52, 53
Phoenicians 8
Popeye Village 74, 108
Pretty Bay 55

Qawra 69

Rabat 64-66, 105
    Grotto of St Paul 64
    Roman Villa Museum 9, 64
    St Agatha's Catacombs 22,
        65, 66

INDEX

St Paul's Catacombs 22, 65
St Paul's Church 64
Ramla Bay (Ramla tat Torri)
 73
Red Tower 73
Rinella Movie Park 109
Romans 9

San Anton Gardens 66, 67
San Anton Palace 67
Second Great Siege 14, 34
Second World War 14, 18, 28,
 31, 68
Senglea (L'Isla) 39, 43-44
 docks 44
 Gardjola Garden 44
 Vedette 43, 44
shopping 104
Skorba temple 75
Sliema 45-46
Spinola Bay 46, 47
Spinola Palace 47
Splash and Fun Water Park
 108
sport 110
St George's Bay 47-48
St Julian's Bay 46-47
St Paul 9, 70-71
St Paul's Bay 70
St Paul's Island 70, 71
St Thomas's Bay (Il-Bajja
 ta'San Tumas) 53

Ta'Ħaġrat 75, 76
Ta'Qali Craft Centre 66, 104

Tarxien Temples 21, 49
Three Cities 24, 39-44
Three Villages 66-69

Valletta 10, 19, 23-38, 93, 113
 Auberge de Castille et León
 25, 27
 Caffe Cordina 34
 Carmelite Church 35
 Casa Rocca Piccola 32
 Church of St Paul Ship-
 wrecked 29, 92
 Fort St Elmo 10, 12, 24, 31,
 108
 Grand Harbour 20, 21, 24
 Grand Master's Palace 32
 Armoury 32
 Apartments 32
 Great Siege Square 36
 In Guardia! 31, 108
 Knights Hospitallers 30, 108
 Lascaris War Rooms 28
 Lower Barracca Gardens 29
 Malta Experience 29-30, 107
 Malta George Cross – The
 Wartime Experience 34,
 108
 Manoel Theatre 35, 109
 market 30
 Mediterranean Conference
 Centre 30
 National Library 35
 National Museum of
 Archaeology 21, 38, 49, 50
 National Museum of Fine

Arts 38
National War Museum 14,
 31
Opera House 25
Palace of the Grand Masters
 20
Queen's Square 34
Republic Square 34
Republic Street (Triq Ir-
 Repubblika) 32
Sacra Infermeria 30
St John's Co-Cathedral 20,
 36-38
 museum 38
Upper Barracca Gardens 28
Valletta Experience 34, 108
Verdala Palace 57-58
Vittoriosa (Birgu) 39, 40-43
 Auberge d'Angleterre 43
 Church of St Lawrence 40
 Fort St Angelo 13, 40
 Freedom Monument 41
 Maritime Museum 42, 43
 Palazzo del Sant'Uffizio
 (Inquisitor's Palace) 41-42

weather 92
Wignacourt Tower 71

Żabbar 48
 Sanctuary of the Virgin of
 Grace 49
Żabbar Gate 48
Żebbug, Church of St Philip
 16